DOGS

BY DESIGN

(HOW TO FIND THE RIGHT MIXED BREED FOR YOU)

Ilene Hochberg

Author of the bestselling books
Dogue, Catmopolitan, Vanity Fur,
and *Good Mousekeeping*

Interlibrary Loan
Development Grant, 2008

STERLING

New York / London
www.sterlingpublishing.com

STERLING and the distinctive Sterling logo are registered trademarks of Sterling Publishing Co., Inc.

Library of Congress Cataloging-in-Publication Data

Hochberg, Ilene, 1955-
  Dogs by design : how to find the right mixed breed for you / Ilene Hochberg.
    p. cm.
  Includes index.
  ISBN-13: 978-1-4027-4354-2
  ISBN-10: 1-4027-4354-8
  1. Dogs. 2. Dog breeds. I. Title.

SF426.H59 2007
636.7—dc22   2007

2   4   6   8   10   9   7   5   3   1

Published by Sterling Publishing Co., Inc.
387 Park Avenue South, New York, NY 10016
© 2007 by Ilene Hochberg
Distributed in Canada by Sterling Publishing
c/o Canadian Manda Group, 165 Dufferin Street
Toronto, Ontario, Canada M6K 3H6
Distributed in the United Kingdom by GMC Distribution Services
Castle Place, 166 High Street, Lewes, East Sussex, England BN7 1XU
Distributed in Australia by Capricorn Link (Australia) Pty. Ltd.
P.O. Box 704, Windsor, NSW 2756, Australia

Book design and layout: Oxygen Design, Tilman Reitzle, Sherry Williams
Photo credits: Cover photos © by Chelle Calbert.
  All formal photographs of Bagel Hounds, Chiweenies, Chugs, Cockaliers, Cock-A-Poos, Faux Frenchbo Bulldogs, Goldendoodles, Labradoodles, Maltipoos, Puggles, Schnoodles, Shihpoos, Taco Terriers, and Yorkipoos © by Chelle Calbert (www.Designerdoggies.com). Pages 7 and 41: Life Magazine cover image © by Jeff Minton / Time & Life Pictures/Getty Images. Page 105 (upper left): Photo © by Jorge Alejandro Preciado Oseguera/SXC. Pages 106, 107 (upper left), 108, 109, 110, 112, 114, 117, 119, 120, 121, and 123: Photos © by Chelle Calbert (www.Designerdoggies.com). Page 107 (lower right): Photo © by iStockphoto.com/Eric Isselée. Page 113 (upper left): Photo © by iStockphoto.com/absolut_100. Page 113 (lower right): Photo © by iStockphoto.com/Erik Lam. Page 116: Photo © by Ken Hurst | Dreamstime.com. Page 118 (bottom right): Photo © by iStockphoto.com/photopix. Page 124: Photo © by Shabina Dalidd | Dreamstime.com.

Printed in China
All rights reserved

Sterling ISBN-13: 978-1-4027-4354-2
          ISBN-10: 1-4027-4354-8

For information about custom editions, special sales, premium and corporate purchases, please contact Sterling Special Sales Department at 800-805-5489 or specialsales@sterlingpub.com.

DEDICATION

For my husband, Bob Wood, who encourages and inspires me.
I love you.

And to the dogs of my memory and heart:
Nubie, Tori, Morgan, Annabel, Bubbles, Suds, Bucky, Mort, Sassy,
Susanna, Charlie, Beanie, and Brownie

CONTENTS

INTRODUCTION
Man-Made Mutts

Mutts are all the rage. That's right. Mixed-breed dogs, once dismissed as lowly mongrels available from the SPCA (Society for the Prevention of Cruelty to Animals), have become our most desirable pets. They are the darlings of the media, with outlets as diverse as the Today Show, the Ellen DeGeneres Show, CNN, The New York Times, The Wall Street Journal, USA Weekend, National Geographic, People, Parade, Life, and most likely your local paper and evening news clamoring to report stories about this new pet phenomenon.

"DESIGNER DOGS," AS THEY ARE COMMONLY CALLED, are being photographed with celebrity owners such as Sylvester Stallone, Uma Thurman, Julianne Moore, Ozzy Osbourne, James Gandolfini, and Jake Gyllenhaal, who all own Puggles, a mix of Pug and Beagle that currently seems to account for 50 percent of the new crossbreeds sought by pet owners. They are joined by Jessica Simpson and Beyonce, who own Malt-A-Poos, a cross between a Maltese and a Poodle; Jennifer Aniston and her Labradoodle, a Labrador Retriever and Poodle hybrid; Natalie Portman and her Schnoodle, a Schnauzer + Poodle mix; and even Queen Elizabeth, whose unplanned Royal Kennel mating of her Corgi and Dachshund created the popular Dorgi. Other celebrities who own mixed-breed dogs of unknown lineage include Hilary Swank, Sheryl Crow, Edie Falco, Zach Braff, Heidi Klum, and Kate Bosworth.

The Puggle (Pug + Beagle) is the most popular of the hybrid mixes. Puggles account for almost half the number of hybrids registered by the American Canine Hybrid Club.

Sadie, the Goldendoodle (Golden Retriever + Poodle) is the Life *Magazine cover dog, illustrating a story on the popularity of hybrids.*

Consumers have come to expect customization in all areas of their lives, from the variety of coffees available at their local Starbucks to the sized-to-order jeans available from retailers such as Levi's and Land's End. We have become accustomed to getting just what we want, when we want it, so it is little surprise that dogs would become the next "product" to be engineered-to-order. "Designer Genes" for the pet set...

New hybrid mixes, created by crossbreeding two breeds of dogs registered by the American Kennel Club (AKC), are providing pet owners with the opportunity to obtain dogs that purport to be allergy-free and not shed, and with the intelligence, size, and personality traits of their purebred parents. It is believed that many of these mixes are healthier than the foundation breeds that created them. The new mixed breeds command high prices and have long waiting lists of people eager to pay for them. Ironically, "mutts" have become the most exclusive dogs on the market today.

Despite the fact that the AKC recognizes 153 breeds of purebred dogs—with five more breeds soon to be added to that list and another 49 breeds in various stages of the certification process—dog owners have created the demand for an additional 372 hybrid mixes, as of the writing of this book (and counting, as the number seems to increase almost daily as people register litters of new mixes). Several mixes even have clubs that disseminate information about their dogs and maintain lists of breeders to promote their creations to the dog-buying public.

Many mixed breeds combine the Poodle with other purebred dogs, aiming to create dogs that do not shed and are allergy-free. The "doodle dogs" include the Labradoodle (Labrador Retriever + Poodle), Goldendoodle (Golden Retriever + Poodle), and Schnoodle (Schnauzer + Poodle). Other Poodle mixes are the Cock-A-Poo (Cocker Spaniel + Poodle), Peke-A-Poo (Pekingese + Poodle), Yorkie-Poo (Yorkshire Terrier + Poodle), and the Shih-Poo (Shih Tzu + Poodle). The Puggle (Pug + Beagle), Cavachon (Cavalier

The Cock-A-Poo (Cocker Spaniel + Poodle) is one of the original hybrid mixes.

King Charles Spaniel + Bichon Frise), and the Zuchon (Shih Tzu + Bichon Frise) round out the top 10 most popular crossbreeds today.

What traits have made these new hybrids so desirable, despite the existence of so many purebred varieties? Which mixed breed is right for you? How do you locate your ideal dog? This book will guide you through the entire process and will answer all the questions you might have while seeking and then living with the dog of your dreams.

When I began to think about writing this book, I had no idea of the highly charged emotions that would be unleashed by a book examining this newly created category of dogs. It was not until I began my research that I became aware of the controversy that surrounds these hybrid dogs. Indeed, proponents of these new mixes—and opponents of them as well—are exceedingly vocal in their opinions regarding the concept of deliberately created mixed-breed dogs.

This is a Zuchon (Shih Tsu + Bichon Frise).

Early in my research, I met Sharon Maguire, who created the popular Web site www.dogbreedinfo.com. It provides visitors with a full range of information about dogs, both purebred and crossbred, and I recommend it as a starting point for potential dog owners who have access to the Internet.

Sharon provided an overview of the mixes popular with pet owners today. Her Web site features descriptions of these mixes and basic information about them as well as photos of dogs posted by visitors to her site. She was kind enough to offer to reach out to the visitors on her site to solicit information and photography of their mixed-breed dogs. She posted an appeal for this information, requesting that people contact me directly at my e-mail address. It all seemed innocent enough....

Within days, my inbox was filled with notes and photo attachments from readers. I could hardly keep up with the flood of responses, so to simplify matters, and to clear my AOL mailbox, I saved all the notes and photos to my computer, planning to read and evaluate the responses when the flurry of mail subsided.

Two weeks later, I began to examine the responses. You can imagine my surprise to find hate mail mixed in with the photos and testimonials to hybrid dogs. People purporting to be supporters of AKC purebred dogs, as well as those in favor of "pound puppies" obtainable through the local animal shelter, sent me angry and threatening notes. Some, who had Googled my name and learned that I had published seven books before this one (many about fashion and pets), questioned my credibility in focusing on a serious topic pertaining to dogs. Comments included the following:

I understand that *you are a fashion writer and are planning a book on so-called designer dogs. DON'T DO IT! If you write this book, you will be doing a terrible disservice to every person you encourage to buy into this SCAM and every parent dog that will suffer in such an irresponsible breeding-for-bucks program, and every puppy born as the result of such a program. You will also ultimately be promoting the production of dogs that will later be discarded into already crowded shelters, where at least half of them will be KILLED because there are not enough adopters.*

"Designer" breeders are simply SCAM artists looking for easy money from foolish customers. They are "P. T. Barnum breeders," expecting that enough fools will fall for the cutesy names that they fasten on their crossbred puppies and that the high prices will fool people into thinking that anything that costly must be worth having.

You are a fashion writer. Instead of writing a useless and damaging book promoting "designer dogs," you might write a useful book concerning how to refurbish one's living quarters to be easy to clean and comfortable for the dog, and how to choose one's clothing to be easy to maintain and practical for living with the dog. A DOG IS NOT A FASHION ACCESSORY. A DOG IS A COMPANION TO BE CHERISHED.

I am a purebred-dog breeder, and hybrids and designer dogs in my opinion are mutts, and their breeders are worse than scum. These are not hybrid or designer dogs…they are crossbred MUTTS!!

This is a Malt-A-Poo, also known as Maltipoo (Maltese + Poodle).

I think it is in very poor taste to support with a book backyard breeders and puppy mills that breed these "mutts" for profit and care nothing about the welfare of the dog. Just what the world needs, "fad" dogs, so that when people get tired of them they can dump them in the street or local shelters. Certainly turns me off and certainly I will not ever recommend your books.

I do not under any circumstances approve of mixed-breeding dogs. That is what the SPCA and rescue are for. As a breeder of purebred dogs, I feel only the best of each breed should go forward or be bred intentionally. Intentionally mixing breeds will result in dogs ending up at the SPCA or rescue centers. I am sorry that you are promoting such a thing.

I breed health-checked, X-rayed PUREBRED dogs with pedigrees and guarantees, and do not support those who breed "designer" mutts for profit. Your book is offensive, and those of us who breed and care about purebred dogs do not breed for fad, fashion, or profit!

I was also the recipient of e-mail from many breeders of hybrid dogs. Here are some of their comments.

Before I submit my info to you, I need to know your credentials... Is this book aimed at "knocking" the crossbreeds or giving both sides to the story? I want to know if my dogs are going to be "put down" before I submit. It is only fair that I know who you are as well, and your intentions. I have been breeding [dogs] for over 10 years, and I am also the founder of NAMC, the North American Malt-A-Poo Club.

We have been lovingly breeding Bichon Frise puppies since 1992. We concentrate on breed standard, health, proper environment, socialization, and nutrition. All our puppies come with health guarantees and shots for life... When my trainer/daughter decided to start her own line of Cavalier King Charles Spaniels, it was natural for us to combine our efforts to create the most wonderful little hybrids, Cavachons.... We are very proud about what we do and take our breeding facility very seriously.

I breed Goldendoodles and love the breed. I am excited to hear that you are writing a book on hybrid and designer breeds. I have looked for a good book on this and cannot find one. I would love to share pictures and information about this breed because I know other people will enjoy Goldendoodles as much as I do.

I have been involved with Labradoodles for three years, two of those as secretary of the International Labradoodle Association. I have been interviewed for a magazine entitled Designer Dogs that is now on the newsstands and for an e-book on Labradoodles that is available online. I own nine breeding dogs; all are also my pets. I do extensive genetic testing in an attempt to ensure my puppies will grow up healthy and sound. My clients are all over the U.S., and I will be sending one puppy to Switzerland shortly....

I bred Labrador Retrievers for seven years prior to falling in love with the Labradoodle. I am happy to say that our puppies go to loving, forever homes. I give a two-year guarantee on any health defects. If for some reason someone is not able to keep his/her puppy and finds it necessary to locate a new home for it, I ask that person to please notify me so that I can have the option of taking the puppy back or helping him/her find it a new home. Under no circumstances do I want any of my puppies turned over to the Humane Society.

I have been breeding dogs since my childhood (my parents own a training and boarding facility and breed Wheatons). I have been breeding Goldendoodles for four years. We currently breed six litters per year. All our dogs are in our home and not kenneled, and we also have a foster program.

I CAME TO REALIZE that the subject of designer dogs is extremely controversial. Opinions are polarized, and people appear to either support or reject the concept with equal vigor. It became my objective as a journalist to present the facts without bias.

According to figures supplied by both the AKC and the American Pet Products Manufacturers Association (APPMA), pets have a home in nearly 63 percent of American households. Forty-five percent of these households have more than one pet. The numbers have increased in recent years; in 1988 only 56 percent of American households owned pets. Of these pet-owning households, 43.5 million own dogs, with a total of 73.9 million dogs sharing their lives with us. This adds up to a large dollar investment, with more than $38.4 *billion* spent on our pets and their care in the last year. Broken down by household, one-time costs such as spaying, neutering, supplies like crates, and so forth, cost pet owners $2,100. Annual costs for the dog's food, grooming, vet check-ups, pet-sitting, and miscellaneous items and services come to an average of $2,500 annually, on a bare-bones budget. That's a lot of money to devote to a pet over the course of his life. And it does not take into account the purchase price of a pure-bred or "designer" pet, which can run into the thousands!

Given all these facts, it's obvious that adding a dog to the family represents a large commitment of emotion, time, and, yes, money. Therefore, it's important to understand what type of dog is right for you—especially when it comes to newer designer dogs, where reliable information can be hard to find. This book will provide you with a clear description of what qualities you can expect to find in a mixed-breed dog. The book will also attempt to debunk the myths, both positive and negative, that surround this new classification of dog. Readers who have interest in locating a dog perfect for their needs will be equipped to make an informed decision about whether a purebred dog, crossbred dog, or dog of indeterminate lineage, found in the local animal shelter, is the best choice for their lifestyle. The only opinion that I will offer is that it is good to have so many options from which to choose. I would expect no less for today's savvy consumer.

The Faux Frenchbo Bulldog (French Bulldog + Boston Terrier) is one of the newer hybrid mixes.

1
The History of the Designer Dog Concept

ONCE UPON A TIME, in the not so recent past, people who wanted to add a dog to their family had several choices. Perhaps the cheapest, and most benevolent, was to go to the local animal shelter to adopt a stray or abandoned dog. Sometimes the shelter would be able to provide information about the breed or possible mix of breeds that had gone into the creation of the dog selected. In many cases, however, the shelter had little definite information about the dog in question. Through observation, they might have been able to venture an educated guess as to the dog's temperament and eventual size, but this was all just speculation. Most dogs acquired from animal shelters were mixed breeds. They were often called "mutts."

Another way to locate a pet was at a local pet store. These shops carried a selection of purebred and mixed-breed dogs. Purebred dogs often came with "papers" from a registry, like the AKC and others, which record the litters of purebred dogs.

Some of the mixed-breed dogs offered for sale were accidentally created when a purebred animal mated with a dog of a different breed or one of unknown lineage. The products of such a mating were commonly referred to as "oops litters." The resulting puppies were crossbreeds and could not be registered by the AKC, which registers only litters derived from two purebred dogs of the same breed. Some crossbred dogs were provided with papers from registries that

The Taco Terrier (Chihuahua + Toy Fox Terrier) sports one of the more imaginative names given to a hybrid mix.

recorded the litters of mixed-breed mating. Many of these mixes were given cute names that were a combination of the names of the breeds of their parents. "Cock-A-Poos" were an early and popular mix that likely originated from the appealing result of such accidental mating.

In most cases, the parents of puppies sold in shops were not at the store. The dogs for sale were often supplied by large-scale breeders, who maintained their breeding animals at their facility and had little if any con-

This is a Schnoodle (Miniature Schnauzer + Poodle).

tact with the person who ultimately bought the pet. As a result, people who bought their pets at a store had to have faith in the store's reputation for providing healthy animals. Their best assurance was to take any puppy considered for purchase to a veterinarian. If a puppy was found to be unhealthy, the person could possibly return the animal to the store for an exchange or a refund.

The third way to find a puppy was to locate one directly from the breeder. This could be accomplished in several ways. The simplest would be to locate a pet through the classified ads in the local paper. Another way would be to go directly to a breeder of your selected breed when referred from a satisfied pet owner. Alternatively, one could contact the AKC or breed club for a list of qualified breeders and locate a breeder from direct research in this way, or by means of a Web site search on the Internet. All these cases might result in an animal with a pedigree and papers from a registry. A visit to the kennel would provide a look at the parents or only the mother of the puppy. Nevertheless, one might have a reasonable idea about the final appearance and temperament of the pet. Examination by a veterinarian was the most reasonable way to assure the pet's health, and most dogs bought from a kennel also came with a health guarantee.

This is a Chug (Chihuahua + Pug).

For many years, these were the established ways to acquire a new dog. People were satisfied with the range of choices available in the broad spectrum of recognized dog breeds or through the mixes that came as a result of accidental interbreeding. Mixed-breed dogs were referred to as "mutts," and were sought out and beloved by many people who could not afford the price of a pedigreed dog, or by those who thought it socially correct to adopt an animal-shelter dog, rather than add to the perceived overpopulation created by the deliberate production and marketing of purebred dogs.

The occasional mix created by an unplanned mating added another choice to the available categories, but this segment was largely sporadic. Even when crossbred combinations were repeated due to the appeal of the resulting mixed-breed puppies, this segment of dogs was only a small component of the total number of dogs available to the dog-seeking public.

Dogs du Jour

THESE DOG-BUYING OPTIONS SUFFICED until one day, people, now called consumers, were exposed to new things. The media, including film, television, magazines, and newspapers, became more pervasive, and persuasive. Suddenly, people who were satisfied with what they had accomplished and acquired in life were being exposed on a more constant basis to people who had more than they did. Much more than they did… "Keeping up with the Joneses" was no longer enough. Now the objective was to keep up with the celebrities beamed daily into their consciousness from a variety of sources.

People began to want the same luxuries available to the elite to whom they were now being exposed in the media. But while stars of film and television screen could afford exotic sports cars, opulent homes, and the perks of fame, like swag bags and the loan of designer wardrobes and jewels, people like you and me were experiencing the ever-increasing pangs of unfulfilled desire. We, too, wanted and deserved the best that life had to offer. Except we had to satisfy that craving on a limited budget.

That is how the market for designer goods was created. Some marketing genius realized that if one applies a famous name, associated with special and wonderful things, to regular stuff, an increased demand for these ordinary items could be created. And, the more mundane, the better.

Virtually overnight, stores became flooded with designer goods: designer clothes, available in stores everywhere from Target to WalMart; designer items for the home (such as those created by Martha Stewart for Kmart); designer ice cream (including Häagen-Dazs and Ben & Jerry's, deliberately positioned by marketing campaigns to be perceived as better and more luxurious than the ice cream brands commonly available in the local supermarket); and even designer coffee (from the likes of Starbucks and Dunkin' Donuts, which has also jumped onto the bandwagon). It seemed as if nothing were exempt from this burgeoning trend. Therefore, it was only a matter of time before the family pet was swept into the fashion frenzy and "designer dogs" were born.

Everyone who is anyone seemed to be seen with her pet in tow. Paris had her Chihuahua, as did Madonna, and Nicole had her Maltese. But not all of us could afford the latest "It Dog." Most of us

This is a Shih Poo (Shih Tzu + Poodle).

had to be satisfied with "Brand X," a dog of unknown or unplanned parentage. "Mutts." How could we (and the breeders attempting to market and sell these dogs) make these simple dogs "fabulous"? Learning from the marketing geniuses, we applied a fashionable name to them: designer dogs.

They were already cute, so how could we make them desirable? The first step in their magnificent transformation was to differentiate the mixes into special groupings, with each mix being assigned a catchy brand name. "Cock-A-Poos" led the way to "Labradoodles," "Goldendoodles," "Puggles," and more. And what better method to achieve media exposure for our newest darlings than to give them the very best PR treatment, pairing them with celebrities and photographing them everywhere. It didn't take long before the lowly "mutt" was transformed into the fabulous "designer dog" that we love and crave today. Ironically, these designer dogs, which began as a way of adding prestige and glamour to the common mixed breed, are now often too pricey for many consumers and have emerged as the new "It Dogs" of today.

If this history seems highly speculative and subjective, well, it is. There is no recorded history of most of these hybrid breeds. What we know comes largely through observation of the trends and social climate of the time during which this new category of dogs has emerged and grown popular. The effect seemed to start small and snowball. The factual basis is rather slim.

A Pup by Any Other Name...

THE AMERICAN CANINE HYBRID CLUB (ACHC; www.achclub.com) is a registry that records the litters of mixed-breed dogs. The club establishes the names of all the new mixed-breed varieties. The rules are simple and egalitarian: The first one to register a litter of a new mix gets to create the name. All subsequent litters and dogs of that mix will be known by that name. The ACHC registers about 500 litters each month, averaging 4.1 puppies per litter. That's a lot of dogs. Currently there are about 369 recognized crossbreeds, and the number increases daily as new combinations are produced and introduced to the dog-buying public.

The registry was created by Garry Garner in 1992 as an offshoot of America's Pet Registry, which had been registering litters of purebred dogs since the 1980s. He and his wife Sheila had been breeders of more than 26 different breeds of dogs. They were early breeders of

Cock-A-Poos, and saw the popularity of that mix firsthand. It can perhaps be stated that with the creation of the American Canine Hybrid Club, the category of deliberately bred mixed-breed dogs was established and granted credibility with the dog-buying public. The concept of the designer dog began to come into its own.

A Visionary Canine Creation

ANOTHER GENESIS OF THE TREND might be traced back to the mid-1970s, when Wally Cochran, a dog breeder at The Royal Guide Dogs in Victoria, Australia, received a special request from a blind woman in Hawaii. Her husband suffered from severe allergies, so she was seeking a guide dog that would not create an allergic reaction. Hair and saliva samples from 33 different poodles bred in Hawaii had been tested, but all aggravated his condition. Could a dog created from foreign stock have more success? She had chosen Australia because it is an island with strict quarantine regulations, so a dog shipped into Hawaii from Australia would be admitted as rabies-free with no delay.

The Labradoodle (Labrador Retriever + Poodle) was first developed in Australia as a guide dog, and is now recognized there as a purebred dog breed.

Cochran suggested a cross between one of their Labrador Retrievers, typically used as guide dogs, and a Standard Poodle, which would lessen the possibility of provoking the man's allergies, because the Poodle's hair does not shed like that of most other breeds. In addition, Poodles are one of the smartest breeds of dog, so introducing the Poodle to the mix could potentially elevate the functionality of the guide dog as well.

There were three puppies in the resulting litter, and one, a dog named Sultan, did not trigger an allergic reaction in the man. Cochran called this first litter "LABRADOr-POODLE," and he shortened the name to "Labradoodle" during an interview he conducted with Channel 9 in Melbourne about "the new breed of guide dog."

Cochran bred Labradoodles to other Labradoodles and called the resulting generation of dogs "Doubledoodles." He next bred the

Doubledoodles to other Doubledoodles, and named their puppies "Tri-Doodles." These new dogs became popular as guide dogs, which ultimately led to indiscriminate breeding in an attempt to fulfill the high demand. In 1989 two breeding facilities, at Rutland Manor and Tegan Park in Victoria, Australia, were established with strict controls. Only health-tested Labradors, Poodles, and third-generation Labradoodles were included in the programs. The breed was improved, and in 1998 breeding was expanded to include Miniature Poodles. The new dogs, called "Miniature Labradoodles," were 14 to 17 inches (35 to 42.5 cm) tall, as compared with the Standard Labradoodle height of 23 to 26 inches (57.5 to 66 cm). When the miniature dogs were crossbred with the standard dogs, a midsize Medium Labradoodle, 18 to 21 inches (45 to 53 cm) tall, was the result.

These Labradoodle variations combine the intelligence and low potential of allergic reaction of the Poodle with the nonaggressive and highly trainable nature of the Labrador. The situation appears to be a win–win, and is said to improve upon the attributes of each of the individual breeds found in the combination. Word of this apparent success may be viewed as the trigger in the creation and popularization of deliberately crossbred dogs.

Hybrid Vigor

AMONG THE FACTORS frequently mentioned in the promotion of deliberately crossbreeding purebred dogs is the theory of *hybrid vigor.* When I began to explore the qualities of the new mixes, the claim of a reduced incidence of genetic defects was offered by nearly every person in support of the new hybrid concept. This benefit was repeated by both hybrid breeders and veterinarians alike. And if you refer back to the simplistic lesson on genetics you received in high-school biology class, you can understand the principles that support this claim.

Unless you are a student of biology or medicine, you may vaguely recall, as I do, something about a monk and experiments with pea plants. A quick Web search for *genetics, pea plants* turned up a paper produced by a geneticist at the Yale–New Haven Teachers Institute. My memory was refreshed as I once again learned that in 1857 an

Austrian monk named Gregor Mendel wondered why in most cases tall pea plants produced tall pea plants while short pea plants produced short pea plants. Once in a while, however, while tall pea plants usually begat tall pea plants, sometimes when crossbred, they would produce short pea plants. Conversely, short pea plants when crossbred usually produced short plants but occasionally begat tall pea plants.

Mendel carefully recorded his plantings and their results, and after time and observation concluded that some inherited traits were dominant and others were recessive. His hypothesis maintained that the dominant traits found in crossbred peas often were exhibited while the recessive traits appeared with lower frequency. Crossbreeding tall plants with short plants would produce only tall plants in the first generation of the mix (see the first table). But if one bred together two of these tall crossbred first-generation "hybrid plants," as he came to call them, the result would likely be in the proportion of three tall plants to one short plant (see the second table). At this time, I more clearly recalled the little boxes we had drawn in school, much like little four-paned windows, to demonstrate why this phenomenon occurred with great predictability.

	T	T
t	Tt	Tt
t	Tt	Tt

This table illustrates the breeding of a tall pea plant (TT) to a short pea plant (tt). This results in the creation of four tall pea plants, all of them hybrids, because they carry the dominant gene for tall plants and the recessive gene for short plants.

	T	t
T	TT	Tt
t	Tt	tt

This table illustrates the breeding of two hybrid tall pea plants. This breeding can create one pure tall pea plant that has no recessive genes, two tall hybrid pea plants, and one short pea plant with two recessive genes.

So, while crossbred pea plants might have resembled one parent pea plant more closely than the other, in actuality each crossed plant contained traits from both parents. If you continued to repeatedly breed the products of such a breeding with each other, you would find a larger proportion of the recessive traits exhibited by the resulting plants.

If you apply this theory to people, you can understand why incest and the marriage of first cousins are forbidden. Beyond the distasteful aspect of "breeding" between close family members, as is deeply ingrained in our conscience by our Judeo-Christian teachings, from a strictly genetic point of view, such a mating would ultimately produce genetic defects that would become dominant, or displayed, from excessive inbreeding. By contrast, recessive defects would remain recessive, or not displayed, in breeding with a partner outside the family.

It is this phenomenon that suggests that repeated inbreeding, that might be done by purebred breeders who might indiscriminately breed genetically defective dogs to other related dogs, creates a manifestation of defects in the resulting puppies. This theory would also suggest that the breeding of two unrelated animals—indeed dogs who do not share any genetic material—would more likely result in pets free from many of their recessive genetic defects. This hypothesis is upheld by hybrid breeders and many veterinarians as well.

The Chiweenie (Chihuahua + Dachshund) is another fanciful name selected for a hybrid mix.

While the theory of hybrid vigor seems to be an ironclad argument for hybrid dogs, it is not the condemnation of purebred dogs that it might appear to be. Responsible breeders of purebred dogs test their animals for signs of disease and remove unhealthy animals from their breeding program. It is only the unscrupulous breeders, who breed dogs solely for profit without caring about the health of their breeding stock or puppies, who are cause for concern.

In addition, the genetic flaws exposed by indiscriminate inbreeding by purebred dog breeders can be replicated over time by hybrid breeders, as they are increasingly breeding their hybrid dogs to other hybrid dogs, in an attempt to create a more predictable result. Therefore, the very argument that supports hybrid vigor is being deliberately abandoned by many hybrid breeders as they strive for the creation of hybrid standards.

Stephanie Shain, director of outreach for companion animals for the Humane Society of the United States (HSUS), explains, "We want consumers to understand that so-called hybrid puppies are not protected from genetic diseases. They are just as likely to have the same problems that other puppies have that come from large-scale, high-volume breeding, especially since the demand is massive and puppy mills are responding by pumping out the hybrid-du-jour as quickly as possible."

Hybrid dogs are often promoted as displaying the best qualities of the two dog breeds that have gone into the mix. While this might be true, in fact such mixed-breed puppies might equally demonstrate the least attractive traits of both parents instead. Predictability in appearance and personality traits is the primary advantage in choosing a purebred dog over a mix, while the hybrids created from two different breeds will produce puppies that may contain any combination of the traits found in both parents. For this reason, it is strongly suggested that you familiarize yourself with all traits found in each dog in the mix. If there is any trait that you find objectionable, steer clear of that combination, because there is no guarantee that you will get the select group of traits you find attractive. This is why we have included a section on the characteristics of the purebred breeds that make up the most popular hybrids.

Pups for Profit?

ONE ARGUMENT PRESENTED against hybrid dogs is that their breeders are strictly motivated by profit, compromising quality in exchange for a high volume of puppies that will increase sales figures. While this might be true of some hybrid breeders, it can also be argued that some purebred breeders are equally profit-oriented and will also stress production over quality. There is no clear argument that one breeder's motives are more "pure" than another's.

"Puppy mills" refer to kennels that breed large quantities of many breeds of dog to fulfill the market demand created predominantly by pet stores. These large-scale kennel operations do not always breed their animals responsibly, neglecting to test for genetic flaws in their breeding stock. In fact, the *New York Times* recently reported that puppy mills and unscrupulous breeders in Japan have been churning out defective dogs at an alarming rate as they attempt to replicate unusual—and profitable—recessive traits through rampant inbreeding. One survey revealed that nearly half of all Labrador retrievers in Japan had suffered from malformed hips. This occurrence is four times higher than in the United States, possibly because some Japanese breeders are seeking more rarified traits that can be reproduced only through inbreeding.

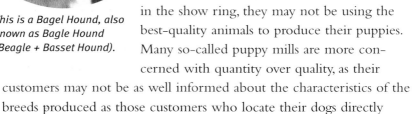

This is a Bagel Hound, also known as Bagle Hound (Beagle + Basset Hound).

In addition, because they are not breeding with the objective of improving the quality of their dogs for potential competition in the show ring, they may not be using the best-quality animals to produce their puppies. Many so-called puppy mills are more concerned with quantity over quality, as their customers may not be as well informed about the characteristics of the breeds produced as those customers who locate their dogs directly from small-scale local breeders specializing in a single breed. Finally, some puppy mills have been sited for maintaining their dogs in poor health and under inhumane conditions.

One breeder of Malt-A-Poos said: "I hope you plan on putting a warning in your book about puppy mills. Because of the huge price of the designer dogs, there are puppy mills out there. Any legitimate breeder of designer dogs should have papers on the puppy through the CKC [Continental Kennel Club] and should allow the customer to visit." However, it should be noted that this unfortunate phenomenon is not limited to breeders of hybrid dogs.

ONE MILLION NEW DOGS are registered with the American Kennel Club (AKC) each year. A simple fact of economics would suggest that all breeders are in the business to produce a profit. To do otherwise would be unproductive and would eventually drive the breeder out of business. There are two ways to produce a profit: by cutting corners and compromising quality, or by investing in the production of the best animals possible, so that the dogs produced will be in great demand and will command the high price that they deserve. Breeders of both purebred dogs and of hybrid dogs can produce a profit

This is a Cockalier (Cocker Spaniel + Cavalier King Charles Spaniel).

in the short run by reducing quality. In time, however, a reputation for poor animals will become known in the industry, ultimately driving them out of business. It is an infinitely better policy to maintain high quality standards and grow the business through success.

Some breeders of purebreds present the argument that all breeders of hybrid dogs are charlatans. While this might be true of unscrupulous breeders of both hybrid and purebred dogs, in truth, most hybrid breeders were once breeders of purebred dogs. Market demands and the breeders' dedication to fulfilling a broader range of expectations have resulted in the creation of the new mixed breeds.

Therefore, hybrid breeders might be perceived as explorers at the forefront of an innovative concept. All things "new" breed suspicion, and the concept of hybrid dogs arouses concern from established breeders of purebred dogs. A better argument might be made that the broader range of offerings will fulfill a larger spectrum of requirements. Customization is the norm in most areas of merchandising, and dog breeding can be perceived as just another industry benefiting from this expanded viewpoint.

Another argument presented against designer dogs maligns the entire concept of designer goods. While some might view the inflated prices of designer goods as unnecessary excess, others embrace the opportunity to purchase something with creative properties at a premium price. The additional fees paid to qualified designers account for the price differential applied to these goods. It can similarly be argued that premium prices are paid to purebred breeders to obtain pedigreed dogs.

The common perception of designer dogs is that they are a premium item and high-priced, like the purebred dogs from which they evolved. The price of a purebred or hybrid dog is higher than the adoption fee for a shelter animal. It is the customer's choice to pay more for what he or she perceives to be a better product. More choices result in more options, which might ultimately drive prices down as increased demands are met by increased production.

One final argument suggests that the popularization of hybrid dogs will result in a population explosion. Hybrid dogs will flood the marketplace, ultimately exceeding demand. The resulting excess dogs will be abandoned, to become the burden of animal shelters, and ultimately be destroyed. Once again, this argument, put forth by both breeders of purebred dogs and the supporters of animals adopted from shelters, is overly simplistic.

According to statistics from the Humane Society of the United States, six to eight million dogs and cats enter shelters every year. The American Society for the Prevention of Cruelty to Animals (ASPCA) puts this figure at eight to 12 million cats and dogs. Both groups are in agreement that 25 percent of the dogs that enter shelters every year are purebreds. Therefore, the advent of adhering to purebred dogs or dogs from random mixing seems to bear little relation to the sheer number of pets who are abandoned to shelters every year.

WHILE THE POPULARITY OF HYBRID DOGS might result in increased supply, in time the supply will match the demand. If the demand falls off, the supply will diminish in response. Hybrid dogs will affect the total dog population neither more nor less than purebred dogs or dogs produced from random mixing. This statement is borne out by the fact that shelter population figures have been rising at the same levels as they have in past years. There has not been a surge in animal abandonment, despite the advent of hybrid dogs, which have only become popular in the past few years. There will always be a demand for dogs that are produced by deliberate design, whether those dogs be purebred or hybrid. People will gravitate toward things that fulfill their unique vision of their needs and desires.

By the same token, there will always be a market for dogs obtained through adoption from animal shelters. Three to four million pets are adopted from shelters each year, according to statistics supplied by both the HSUS and the ASPCA. Some shelter dog customers will be responsive to the altruistic mission of providing a home to a stray dog, while others will be economically motivated by the lower price associated with the acquisition of a dog from a shelter, as compared with the greater purchase price of an animal obtained from a store or a breeder.

So, perhaps the best way to evaluate the dog most suited to your needs is to examine your requirements. Are you motivated by price? Are you seeking something exclusive or unique? Do you have medical issues that must be addressed through your choice of animal? Do you value predictability enough to pay a premium price for that assurance? Will an established dog breed meet all your needs, or do you seek a combination of traits not found in any one breed? Can you embrace all of a dog's potential qualities? Do you believe in saving the world, one homeless dog at a time?

After you have defined exactly what you want and need, you must ask yourself whether a purebred dog, a hybrid dog, or a dog of indeterminate lineage will best satisfy your desires. Only then can you determine if a designer dog is the right pet for you. While this is a question involving many factors, the short quiz below will get you started.

Another example of a Puggle.

Is a Hybrid Dog the Right Dog for You?

IS A HYBRID DOG the right fit for you, or are you better off with a pound puppy or purebred pup? Here are a few questions to consider:

1. Is there an allergy sufferer in your family?

    ○ Yes (2)   ○ No (1)

2. Are you prepared to pay a large sum of money to purchase a dog?

    ○ Yes (2)   ○ No (1)

3. Would you prefer to adopt a dog?

    ○ Yes (0)   ○ No (2)

4. Do you like to be the first to do something new?

    ○ Yes (1)   ○ No (0)

5. Is your choice of dog a reflection of who you are?

    ○ Yes (2)   ○ No (1)

6. Must your dog conform to a predictable set of traits?

    ○ Yes (3)   ○ No (0)

7. Is this your first dog?

    ○ Yes (2)   ○ No (0)

Score: Add up the points in parenthesis after your selected answer.

INTERPRETING THE RESULTS

3–6 points: Pound Puppy
Those scoring in this range would do well to consider a dog of indeterminate lineage, which could include shelter dogs or sometimes dogs from a store. To find such a dog, contact your local humane society or your local veterinarian, or look for adoption ads in the local newspaper and posted in public places like the bulletin boards at pet stores, veterinary offices, schools, and supermarkets.

7–12: Designer Dog or Purebred Pup
Either a hybrid or a purebred dog could be the dog for you. Both dogs offer a level of prestige and exclusivity. Purebred dogs add a measure of predictability to what physical characteristics and behavioral traits you can expect to see in your dog. Hybrid dogs offer less predictability, as they can resemble either parent dog breed in an unknown combination of traits. It is best when considering a hybrid dog that you learn all the traits of the two dog breeds that combined to produce your potential pet. Only if you can live happily with all of these qualities, in any random combination, should you consider the selection of a hybrid dog.

13–14: Purebred Pooch
You should consider restricting your options to purebred breeds. With these breeds, you can be fairly confident in your dog's traits, including temperament, the size it will grow to, and, for allergy sufferers, whether or not the dog will shed. For details on specific breeds, see chapter 3.

What Characteristics Are You Looking for in a Dog?

NOW THAT YOU'VE TAKEN A MOMENT to analyze whether a purebred, hybrid, or mixed-breed dog is right for you, let's focus on the qualities you're looking for in a dog. These desired characteristics will come into play as you read about the different hybrids and the breeds that create them.

PART 1: SIZE

1. Where do you live?

- ○ City (1)
- ○ Suburb (2)
- ○ Country (3)

2. Will you have time to exercise your dog?

- ○ Seldom (1)
- ○ Sometimes (2)
- ○ Frequently (3)

3. Do you have children?

- ○ No (3)
- ○ Young children (1)
- ○ Older children (2)

4. Are you looking for a

- ○ Small dog? (1)
- ○ Medium dog? (2)
- ○ Large dog? (3)

5. Is your dog for

- ○ Companionship? (1)
- ○ Some protection? (2)
- ○ Guard dog? (3)

6. Are you an experienced dog owner?

- ○ Yes (3)
- ○ No (1)

INTERPRETING THE RESULTS

6 POINTS OR LESS:
Good Things Come in Small Packages
Your lifestyle dictates a small dog would be the right fit for you. Popular small dogs include any of the popular toy breeds, or hybrids that incorporate a toy dog or two into the mix. See the list of purebred dogs in chapter 3 to learn more about your choices.

7–14 POINTS: **Small and Medium-Size Dogs Only**
If you prefer, you may add a medium-size dog to your list of options. Popular medium-size breeds include most of the Terriers, some of the Hounds and Spaniels, many dogs like Miniature Poodles or Bichon Frises, and any mix that includes dogs such as these in the breeding.

15 POINTS OR MORE: **Any Size You Please**
Small, medium, and large dogs are all options for you. Looking to supersize your canine companion? Popular big breeds include Labrador Retrievers, Golden Retrievers, German Shepherds, Newfoundlands, Great Danes, and many of the larger Hounds and Spaniels, as well as any hybrids that include these large dogs in the combination.

PART 2: OTHER CONSIDERATIONS

1. Are you willing to spend time grooming your dog daily? Weekly? Monthly?

IF YOU ARE WILLING to groom your dog daily, you are a candidate for a longhaired dog, such as a Yorkie, Maltese, Shih Tzu, or a hybrid dog that includes these breeds in the mix. For weekly grooming, consider a medium-haired dog, such as many of the Terriers, Retrievers, and Spaniels. If you're looking to groom your dog monthly, a shorthaired dog may be your best bet. Such dogs include Pugs, Bulldogs, Boxers, Shorthair Dachshunds, Chihuahuas, and Fox Terriers.

2. Is there an allergy sufferer in your family?

If yes, then choose a breed that doesn't shed, such as a Poodle, Bichon Frise, or a hairless dog like the Chinese Crested. Also, as mentioned earlier, a purebred or hybrid dog may be best for allergy sufferers. Select from breeds or mixes that typically do not shed or release dander.

3. Are you an experienced dog owner?

If this is your first dog, you probably are not accustomed to canine grooming. As such, again, a non-shedding purebred or hybrid may be the right fit for you, as well as a small or medium-size dog, which may be easier to train for someone inexperienced with these animals.

4. Do you prefer a male or a female dog?

Some people prefer a female dog, because they are more maternal and nurturing, and will not mark furniture in the house, making them easier to housebreak. Male dogs are preferred by those who value the watchdog/ guard dog aspect of a pet. They tend to be more aggressive than female dogs and so might be a more effective deterrent against danger. They can also be more difficult to train, both in terms of housebreaking and obedience. However, these characteristics are just a select few of the complete traits of your dog, and should not be the sole determining factors when making your selection of a pet. Both male and female dogs make wonderful companion animals.

Poochons (Poodle + Bichon Frise) are especially good for people who suffer from allergies.

These are Yorkipoos (Yorkshire Terrier + Poodle).

YOU SHOULD NOW HAVE AN IDEA whether a purebred, hybrid, or mixed-breed dog is the best one for you. You should also have an indication as to your preferred dog size and hair length, to narrow down your decision. Those seeking a dog that will not affect allergy sufferers should choose one that doesn't shed (such as Poodles and hairless breeds). Finally, you may have a preference for a male or female dog.

If you would like further information on which dog breeds are best for your needs, visit the Web site www.dogbreedinfo.com and click on "Find the Perfect Dog!" Next, click on "Take the Breed Selector Quiz." After a few simple questions, the program will provide you with a detailed list of dog breeds that may be perfect for your needs. You can also click on the other "Find the Perfect Dog!" categories for additional and more-detailed information.

2
Twenty Popular Designer Dogs

Hybrid dogs can be products of unplanned breeding or created by deliberate design. Regardless of the inciting incident, both methods will result in a dog that is a mix of breeds, be it a random mix of unknown origin or a mix of two purebred breeds. For the sake of this book, we will be examining those dogs created from two purebred parents of different breeds.

UNLIKE PUREBRED DOGS, hybrid mixes are not produced with absolute predictability as to appearance and behavior. They can resemble either of the dog breeds that went into the mix, or can have a combination of traits from both breeds, in any proportion. The best thing to do before thinking about adding a hybrid-mix dog to your home and family is to familiarize yourself with all the characteristics of both breeds that go into your chosen mix. This includes size, activity level, intelligence, personality, coat type, appearance, temperament, and any other aspects of the two breeds in question.

Are you able to embrace all of these traits, or do you find some objectionable? If you do find traits that do not appeal to you, please consider another dog, be it purebred or mixed. The thing to remember is that while you might get a puppy with all of the qualities that you find most appealing, it is equally possible to get a puppy that exhibits all of the unpleasant aspects of both parents' breeds.

Because these dogs are bred from two unlike breeds of dogs, there is generally no breeding program to produce predictability within the resulting litters. To do so would nullify one of the fundamental arguments in favor of hybrid mixes over purebred dogs: hybrid vigor (see page 20 in chapter 1). This method of preventing the spread of undesirable traits is accomplished only through a mix of disparate genes, which would no longer be the case if these mixes were inbred for consistency. To do this would replicate the process used to create purebred dogs. The resulting puppies would be equally likely to exhibit the flaws found from inbreeding as purebred dogs bred in the same manner.

In the pages that follow, you'll find photographs, facts, and opinions from owners and breeders of 20 of the most popular hybrid mixes. The first five hybrids presented represent the top five most popular, according to the American Canine Hybrid Club. We then explore 15 additional popular mixes, presented in alphabetical order.

As discussed, the best way to predict the traits of your mixed-breed puppy is to understand the traits of both foundation breeds, and realize that you will obtain any random combination of these qualities along the spectrum of possibilities. Therefore, unlike conventional books that describe the qualities of your chosen breed of dog, the best I can offer is to tell you which two breeds went into that particular mix, and then refer you to the next chapter of the book, which briefly describes each of the purebred breeds that go into these popular mixes. It is up to you to put together the entire picture. It's kind of like a menu in a Chinese restaurant: Choose one from column A and one from column B....

You may also work this backward: You can read the traits of each of the purebred dogs and then select the two you like best as the foundation for your own custom-blended dog. In Appendix A, "A Complete Listing of Hybrid Breeds," you'll find a list of all the hybrid dogs registered with the American Canine Hybrid Club, organized by the parent breeds.

While reading about the traits of each of the purebred dogs, you might also discover that one breed suits all your needs. In this case, I would advise that you abandon your idea of finding a hybrid puppy and choose a purebred one instead.

> **Metric Equivalents**
> *1 inch = 2.54 centimeters (cm)*
> *1 pound = 0.45 kilogram (kg)*

Finally, if all of this becomes too complicated, or if you find yourself turned off by the complex machinations of finding either a purebred or hybrid puppy, I advise you to do the socially correct thing. Go to your local animal shelter to adopt a puppy and reduce by one the overpopulation of homeless dogs. The choice is ultimately yours.

Puggle

• PARENT BREEDS •

Pug

Beagle

• DOG DATA •

THIS MIX ACCOUNTS for more than 50 percent of the new hybrids registered by the American Canine Hybrid Club. This popularity may be due to the visibility of celebrity Puggle owners, including Sylvester Stallone, Uma Thurman, Julianne Moore, Ozzy Osbourne, James Gandolfini, and Jake Gyllenhaal. Based on its parent breeds, the Puggle may range from 10 to 15 inches (25 to 37.5 cm) in height and may weigh between 14 and 30 pounds (6.3 and 13.5 kg). Both parent breeds have a short coat. While the Beagle is of average intelligence and not particularly obedient, breeding it with the highly intelligent and eager-to-please Pug can potentially yield a Puggle puppy that is easier to train than its Beagle parent. The Puggle is generally child-friendly and not recommended for allergy sufferers. See pages 106 and 117 for more information on Beagles and Pugs.

Meet my two beautiful Puggles. The puppies are male and from the same litter. Digger's traits seem to be taking more after the Pug. He has a wrinkled face, but his nose is a bit longer, like a Beagle. He doesn't seem to have trouble breathing as normal Pugs do. Copper looks more like a Beagle; his color and markings are from the Beagle side. Both of my puppies have curly tails and ears shaped like a Pug's. Digger weighs about 20 pounds [9 kg], and Copper weighs about 22 pounds [10 kg]. Copper is taller than Digger, and both dogs seem to have longer feet and legs than those of regular Pugs. It is exciting to see them change and grow."

—Bunny P.

My Puggle Riley

is very sweet-natured and affectionate. As a young puppy, he was very energetic. As he matures, he's getting calmer, although still game for playtime or a walk. Last spring I got another Puggle, Josie. Josie's birthday was January 29, 2006, so she's going on seven months old. Similar to Riley, she is very sweet-natured, and perhaps a bit more of an explorer.—Sharon M.

Gordon, a brindle-colored Puggle, six months old now, is a mix of a male Pug and a female Beagle. I purchased Gordon from a couple in Vancouver, Washington, who had purchased two Puggles and decided they could not handle them both. I am a bit biased, I'm sure, but Gordon is a pretty handsome boy. He's got the Beagle body and tail, but has that distinctive Pug smile (a cute underbite). And he smiles a lot.—Jay V.

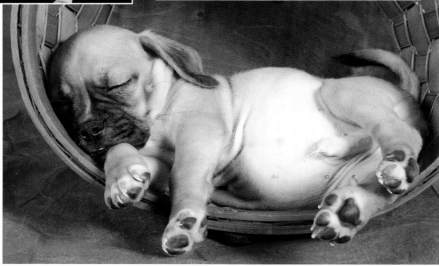

Goldendoodle

• PARENT BREEDS •

Golden Retriever

Poodle

• DOG DATA •

LINDA ROGERS, OF TIMSHELL FARM (www.timshellfarm.com),
a breeder of Goldendoodles (whose dog Sadie
appeared on the cover of *Life* magazine for the story
"The Perfect Dog?"), describes the Goldendoodle
this way:

> The size and color of the puppies depend upon
> the size and colors of the parent dogs' back-
> grounds. Golden Retrievers vary in coat shades
> from light to medium golden to copper red.
> Poodle coats can be white, cream, apricot,
> golden, red, chocolate, or black. Goldendoodle
> puppies usually have a poodle-like coat but not the wiry,
> stiff curls. The texture can be curly—either in tight curls or slightly
> curly, or just plain silky. Goldendoodle size is determined mainly by
> the Poodle parent being either a Standard or Miniature Poodle. Since
> this is a hybrid and not a "standardized breed," it is important to note
> that specific sizes cannot be guaranteed for grown dogs. Buyers must
> be willing to accept that a puppy will likely grow to be within the
> weight ranges of the parent breeds [approximately 12 to 75 pounds
> (5.4 to 34 kg)].

Goldendoodles combine the wonderful traits of both the Golden Retriever
and Poodle purebreds, and these characteristics can include the following:

• Loyal	• Easy to train	• Great desire to please
• Intelligent	• Affectionate	• Probable low to no shedding
• Gentle	• Sunny disposition	• Allergy reduction or elimination

Most Goldendoodles shed very little or not at all, and as a result, may
not cause allergies. There is no guarantee that a Goldendoodle puppy
will be completely "shedless" or will not produce allergies, but it is likely.

See pages 110 and 115 for more information on Golden Retrievers
and Poodles.

Our little Annie is a *Goldendoodle, and especially beautiful. My wife's grandfather raised a different breed of dog, so she has been around a lot of different dog personalities. My wife says that she has never encountered a dog with as much love or spirit as Annie. She loves everybody and everything; she just loves being alive....She was born with her nine brothers and sisters on May 13, 2005. She has grown to 49 pounds [22 kg] now, and she still draws a lot of attention; the novelty of her has not worn off. Even the tough young guy in the neighborhood coos, "Just the cutest little puppy in the world," as we walk by.—Art and Karen R.*

My dog Charlie is a *female Goldendoodle. I picked her up from a breeder in Virginia. She is currently 10 months old, very smart, and a quick learner. I am a very proud parent.—Linn T.*

I am the proud owner of a Goldendoodle named Maggie. Maggie is the product of a Golden Retriever bred to a Standard Poodle. I love my Maggie doodle so much and had such a hard time finding her that I have decided to breed Goldendoodles myself.—Audra M.

Murphy is a Goldendoodle. His mother is a Standard Poodle and his father is a Golden Retriever. The couple we purchased him from are not professional breeders; they just had two dogs they thought were wonderful and decided to breed them. They didn't know they had produced Goldendoodles until their veterinarian told them. Murphy is now almost two years old and is a certified search-and-rescue dog with American Search Dogs. He regularly rides on the back of our ATV. We do demonstrations for scouts and schools to teach children how to approach strange dogs. We also visit assisted-living facilities, where he is gentle with the older residents. He is always the center of attention.—Paulette B.

My dog Rickey

is a Goldendoodle…one year and nine months old. Ricky is a wonderful dog. He is super-friendly and intelligent. He is a quick learner; you can almost see his brain trying to figure things out. He sheds very little. He loves people, especially little girls. He loves dogs as well. He is very docile but can be vocal when he wants something.
—Marilyn M.

My Goldendoodle

Sam is nonshedding, smart, healthy, and has a wonderful personality.—Sam's "mom"

I started breeding dogs in 1987 and started with Goldendoodles in 2001. I have had about 40 litters to date....As you may know, the Goldendoodle has become wildly popular because it is a fun-loving, easygoing, warm and fuzzy friend. The other great benefit is its low- or no-shed coat quality, which makes cleaning the house a breeze.—Michael W.

Labradoodle

• PARENT BREEDS •

Labrador Retriever

Poodle

• DOG DATA •

THIS MIX ORIGINATED IN AUSTRALIA almost 30 years ago and gained fame after being toted around by celebrity owner Jennifer Aniston. Labradoodles range in size and weight, depending on whether the Poodle parent is a miniature or standard breed. Labradors are generally not good pets for allergy sufferers; however, because Poodles are one of the best breeds for those with allergies, Labradoodles may not shed as much as Labrador Retrievers. This is difficult to predict, as the dog may resemble the Labrador in this aspect and may shed as much as the purebred does.

Our dog Jack is a full-size black Labradoodle. He is so good with anyone around him....He is gentle, loving, caring, smart, and so handsome. I will only say one thing we didn't expect is that Jack sheds a lot. You can get a Labradoodle that doesn't shed at all or one that sheds a lot. I have noticed that the Labradoodles that have the curlier hair shed less.—Cindi C.

Both parent breeds boast high intelligence, with the Poodle being one of the most intelligent dog breeds, and Labradoodles are generally good with children. For the specific qualities of the Labrador Retriever and the Poodle, see pages 111 and 115.

Grizwald, the chocolate Labradoodle with the gorgeous green eyes, was named that because he looks like a big grizzly bear. Grizwald is as sweet and well-behaved as they come. He is smart, playful, and attentive. He loves people and follows us wherever we go. While he does have a nonshedding coat, that doesn't mean that he is mess-free! His goatee gets soaked in water whenever he drinks, and he is a leaf and brush magnet. I personally find all of these things absolutely adorable, though. He is a cuddler and has absolutely brightened up my life.
—Emily B.

Kairi is a red apricot Labradoodle—half Standard Poodle and half Labrador Retriever. She is the best dog I have ever had. She is smart, loving, and such a clown, and what a personality she has! I have never had a dog with this much personality before. I love her to death.—Brittany V.

Cock-A-Poo

(Also spelled "Cockapoo")

• PARENT BREEDS •

Cocker Spaniel

Poodle

• DOG DATA •

THIS COMBINATION WAS PERHAPS THE FIRST deliberately bred mix in this country, after accidental breeding created desirable puppies. As with the other "doodle dogs," the size and weight of the Cock-A-Poo varies, depending on whether its Poodle parent is a toy, miniature, or standard breed. Both the Cocker Spaniel and the Poodle are good with kids and possess above-average intelligence. Cocker Spaniels have medium-length coats and therefore are not recommended for allergy sufferers; however, because of the Poodle's no-shed coat, owners and breeders often cite the Cock-A-Poo as being more hypoallergenic than the Cocker Spaniel. Whether or not your Cock-A-Poo will shed is unpredictable. See pages 107 and 115 for more on Cocker Spaniels and Poodles.

My wife and I rescued our Cock-A-Poo Simon from the aftermath of Hurricane Katrina. I believe him to be about three-and-a-half years old. He nearly died of heartworm disease. Born with juvenile cataracts, he was blind when we found him. He had survived alone for two months without sight in an environment that totally changed [on] the day of the hurricane. We had his vision restored. Ironically, his sight was returned to him on the one-year anniversary of the hurricane. He is the most lovable pet we've known. He has demonstrated an uncanny will to live. He has changed our lives as much as we have changed his.—W. J. J.

This is my

Cockapoo Toby. He is 12 weeks old. My family loves him to pieces and we think he is the sweetest dog ever! He is a wonderful lap dog. He gets along with all cats and dogs... Anything he meets is instantly his best friend. He is a beautiful example of the breed and has a temperament to match!—Courtney M.

We run a small family kennel with eight female Cocker Spaniels, two male Cocker Spaniels, and two male Miniature Poodles for crossbreeding Cockapoos. We primarily raised Cockers, but Cockapoos are much better for people with allergies. We have been dealing with the AKC with the Cockers, but as you know, the hybrids will be listed with the Canine Kennel Club.—Joyce S.

We have had many litters of Cockapoos—
good mix, good family dog, although they can be bossy
with kids and treat them as siblings. They need
guidance through the puppy stages. Usually
hypoallergenic.—*Renée B. and Sherwood P.*

Cavachon

• PARENT BREEDS •

Cavalier King Charles Spaniel

Bichon Frise

• DOG DATA •

LINDA ROGERS, OF TIMSHELL FARM
(www.timshellfarm.com), describes their
Cavachons: A Timshell Cavachon puppy has
a Bichon Frise mother and a Cavalier King
Charles Spaniel sire. Our puppies will be
either white or two-colored, with the buff or
copper masks and markings. These specialty hybrid puppies have
the following traits from their parent dogs:

- The low- to nonshedding, nonallergenic coat of the Bichon
- The Bichon's energy and playful nature
- The sweet, friendly temperament of the Cavalier
- The rich coat colors and variations of the Cavalier
  with the soft coat of the Bichon
- People-loving personality
- High intelligence
- Stronger health than either purebred

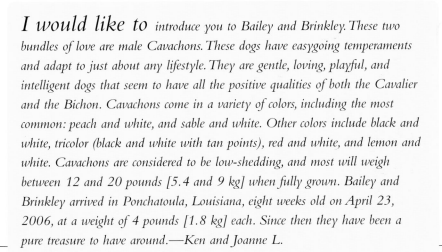

FOR MORE INFORMATION, see page 103 (Bichon
Frise) and page 105 (Cavalier King Charles Spaniel).

I would like to introduce you to Bailey and Brinkley. These two
bundles of love are male Cavachons. These dogs have easygoing temperaments
and adapt to just about any lifestyle. They are gentle, loving, playful, and
intelligent dogs that seem to have all the positive qualities of both the Cavalier
and the Bichon. Cavachons come in a variety of colors, including the most
common: peach and white, and sable and white. Other colors include black and
white, tricolor (black and white with tan points), red and white, and lemon and
white. Cavachons are considered to be low-shedding, and most will weigh
between 12 and 20 pounds [5.4 and 9 kg] when fully grown. Bailey and
Brinkley arrived in Ponchatoula, Louisiana, eight weeks old on April 23,
2006, at a weight of 4 pounds [1.8 kg] each. Since then they have been a
pure treasure to have around.—Ken and Joanne L.

Bagel Hound

(Also spelled "Bagle Hound")

• PARENT BREEDS •

Basset Hound

Beagle

• DOG DATA •

THE BAGEL HOUND MAY RANGE from 13 to 15 inches (32.5 to 37.5 cm) in height and from 18 to 60 pounds (8 to 27 kg), based on its parent breeds. Both parent breeds have short coats, and neither is recommended for allergy sufferers. Bagel Hounds are typically good with children, but may be difficult to train.

For more on the Basset Hound and the Beagle, see pages 101 and 102.

There's something definitely all-American about seeing fellow residents enjoying the summer breeze, kids playing in the grass and slurping a snow cone. We took our dog, a Basset-Beagle mix (our Bagel), and she was the hit of the party. It's easy to make friends with a tortilla-eared, enthusiastic hound by your side.
—*Libby, posted on a south Texas community blog*

Boglen Terrier

• PARENT BREEDS •

Beagle

Boston Terrier

• DOG DATA •

BASED ON ITS PARENT BREEDS, the Boglen Terrier may range in height from 13 to 17 inches (32.5 to 42.5 cm) and in weight from 15 to 30 pounds (7 to 13.5 kg). Both parent breeds have short coats, and neither is recommended for allergy sufferers. While the Beagle can be difficult to train, the Boston Terrier is very intelligent, potentially resulting in a Boglen Terrier puppy that is easier to train than its Beagle parent. Both breeds are good with children.

For more on the Beagle and the Boston Terrier, see pages 102 and 104.

My six-year-old Boglen Terrier has the most wonderful disposition and is truly the best dog I have ever owned. She knows when to play and when it's time to calm down. She is very quiet, only sounding off her Beagle call when she's frightened. She is wonderful with my children and puts up with almost anything. She has no health problems of any kind.—Angela H.

Bosey came from a pet store in Buffalo Grove, Illinois. We couldn't resist her cuteness. Her mom was a 16-pound [7.2-kg] Beagle and her dad was a 10-pound [4.5-kg] Boston Terrier. She weighed a little over 3 pounds [1.35 kg] when we got her at eight weeks. Now she weighs about 20 pounds [9 kg] at one year old. She is the perfect mix between the two dogs. She has the eyes of the Boston Terrier, the snout and nose of the Beagle (we can't let her off the leash because she will follow a scent trail), and the ears are a mix between the two. She is brindle in color, with white on her neck, the bottom portion of her paws, and her belly. Luckily, she did not inherit the Beagle howl. Bosey is full of energy and loves to go to the dog park just about every day to run and play with the big dogs. She loves all people and gets very excited when any person or animal is around. She is strong-willed and smart and knows many tricks, which she will happily do for a treat! She is a lot of work, but she has brought us a lot of happiness.—Shannon B. and Foy S.

Chiweenie

• PARENT BREEDS •

Chihuahua

Dachshund

• DOG DATA •

THE CHIWEENIE MAY GROW to be between 5 and 9 inches (12.5 and 22.5 cm) in height. Its weight varies, depending on whether it has a Miniature or Standard Dachshund parent. Both parent breeds are bright, although the Dachshund is of average obedience. However, the Chihuahua is typically easy to train, and may bestow this characteristic upon its Chiweenie puppy. Both parents are good with children, and neither is recommended for allergy sufferers. See pages 106 and 108 for more on the Chihuahua and the Dachshund.

How can you not smile when you say "Chiweenies?"
—*Blogger*

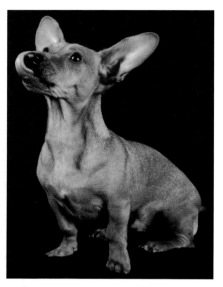

One of the Swanky Pooches in my family is a Chiweenie. His name is Buddy, and he's a little over a year old. We found him in the local newspaper; I wanted to adopt a shelter dog. Unfortunately, I couldn't find anything that met our strict requirements. Buddy is a great little guy, full of energy and so happy. There's just something about that cute little face and cockeyed ear that makes me smile every time I see him. So while I don't endorse the breeding and sale of high-priced "designer dogs," I certainly am happy that someone bred my sweet little Chiweenie!—From a posting on the Swanky Pooch (www.swankypooch.com)

Nyles is a year-old Chiweenie mix pup. He is 15 pounds [7 kg] of adorable love! Nyles is okay with other dogs, but we think he would do best as a single dog or with one doggie companion. While Nyles is good with humans, young children tend to overwhelm him, so we're looking for an adult household for Mr. Nyles. THIS DOG IS TOO COOL FOR SCHOOL! E-mail xxxx for more information on this cute-as-a-button bundle of cute stuff!
—From an ad for a Chiweenie available for adoption, posted on the Internet on Craig's List in San Francisco

63

Chug

• PARENT BREEDS •

Chihuahua

Pug

• DOG DATA •

CHUGS ARE RELATIVELY SMALL dogs, growing from 6 to 18 inches (15 to 45 cm) in height and up to 18 pounds (8 kg), based on the parent breeds. Both parent breeds are highly intelligent, easy to train, and good with children. Neither is recommended for allergy sufferers. See pages 106 and 107 for more on the Chihuahua and the Pug.

My dog Chuggie is a very good example of the Chug hybrid. He is affectionate, friendly, and very eager to please.—Matt B.

My dog Boomer is a Chug. He is two years old and I adopted him from a no-kill shelter at the age of seven months. Boomer is a great mixture of the two breeds. He grunts, snorts, and purrs like a Pug, with his cute Pug tail, while at the same time he's prone to get shaky and extremely nervous in situations he should already be used to (such as car rides and swimming).—Maria G.

Cockalier

• PARENT BREEDS •

Cocker Spaniel

Cavalier King Charles Spaniel

• DOG DATA •

THE COCKALIER MAY GROW to between 12 and 15½ inches (30 and 39 cm) in height and between 13 and 28 pounds (6 and 12.6 kg), based on its parent breeds. Both parents have medium-length silky coats, and neither is recommended for allergy sufferers. Owners consistently praised this mix's intelligence, which may be the result of the above-average intelligence of both parent breeds. For more on the Cavalier King Charles Spaniel and the Cocker Spaniel, see pages 105 and 107.

Otis, our 10-month-old Cockalier, has a great disposition, loves to swim, and is very playful with children. Our dog is pretty big, weighing over 30 pounds [13.5 kg] at 10 months. He recently got a "sporty Cocker" haircut, because the groomer felt that his body shape was more Cocker than Cavalier. I notice that other Cockaliers have long hair like a Cavalier.—Colleen D.

My dog Nigel is a Cockalier. Nigel is a very smart and friendly dog. He knows all his different toys by name and learns tricks within a day or two. He loves to swim. I can't keep him out of water in the summer! He weighs a bit under 30 pounds [13.5 kg]. —Lauren R.

Faux Frenchbo Bulldog

• PARENT BREEDS •

Boston Terrier

French Bulldog

• DOG DATA •

BASED ON ITS PARENT BREEDS, the Faux Frenchbo Bulldog may grow to be 11 to 17 inches (27.5 to 42.5 cm) in height and from 15 to 28 pounds (6.75 to 12.6 kg). Both parents have short coats, and neither is recommended for allergy sufferers. Both parents are good with children. While the French Bulldog is of average intelligence, the Boston Terrier's higher intelligence may result in a Faux Frenchbo Bulldog puppy that is easier to train than its Bulldog parent. For specific characteristics of the Boston Terrier and the French Bulldog, see pages 104 and 109.

This mix is so new that there is no information currently available on the Internet (as of the writing of this book). In time, however, more information may materialize. This is a liability of being "the first one on your block" to desire the newest hybrid dog.

Lhasa Poo

• PARENT BREEDS •

Lhasa Apso

Poodle

• DOG DATA •

THE LHASA POO VARIES IN SIZE, depending
on whether the Lhasa Apso is bred with a Toy,
Miniature, or Standard Poodle. While the
Lhasa Apso is not typically recommended for
allergy sufferers, breeding it with a Poodle, one
of the best dogs for those who suffer from allergies, may result in a Lhasa Poo puppy that is hypoallergenic. Similarly, the high intelligence of the Poodle may make the
Lhasa Poo easier to train than its Lhasa Apso parent. See pages 112 and
115 for more information on the Lhasa Apso and the Poodle.

My dog, Coco Chanel,
is a two-year-old Lhasa Poo. She was
given to me when she was about four
months old. She is a wonderful dog.
She sits in the window when I am
not at home and waits for me to
return. She follows me all over the
house. She's very smart. She brings
me her leash when she wants to go
outside.—Robin M.

My Lhasa Poo's
name is Wrigley. Her body is
like a Poodle, with the face and
ears of a Lhasa.—Joseph L.

71

Malt-A-Poo

(Also spelled "Maltipoo")

Maltese

Poodle

• DOG DATA •

MALT-A-POO OWNERS PRAISE their dogs as highly intelligent and easy to train. Their size and weight ranges, depending on whether the Poodle parent is a Toy or a Miniature (although, generally, Toy Poodles are used for this mix). Both parent breeds are typically recommended for allergy sufferers. For specific characteristics of the Maltese and the Poodle, see pages 113 and 115.

Maverick is a six-month-old
6-pound [2.7-kg] Maltipoo (half Toy Poodle, half Maltese). I adopted Maverick from a breeder in Terrell, Texas. He is extremely smart, loving, and playful, but also stubborn.—Christine P.

My Maltipoo has straight black hair. Before I got her, I looked all over the Internet for pictures of Maltipoos, and I never saw one like her, so I think it would be helpful for people to see as many possibilities of the mix as possible. I know that would have been helpful for me.—Danielle D.

I have a white female

Maltipoo named Lucy. She is six months now and so far very easy to train. She has an outgoing personality and is always interested in everything that is going on around her. Lucy loves to play with other dogs and is constantly running around the house. She is a good dog to travel with because she sits nicely in the car and sometimes even falls asleep! I got Lucy from a breeder that I found on dogbreedinfo.com. The breeder had a white male Maltese, and the mother was an apricot Poodle. Lucy is 8 1/2 pounds [4 kg] now and will probably grow to be 9 or 10 pounds [4 or 4.5 kg] at the most. She is so adorable!—Sara G

Peke-A-Poo

(Also spelled "Peek-A-Poo" and "Peekapoo")

• PARENT BREEDS •

Pekingese

Poodle

• DOG DATA •

THE PEKE-A-POO CAN RANGE in height from 6 to 9 inches (15 to 22.5 cm) and generally weighs less than 14 pounds (6.3 kg). It can be independent and difficult to train, like the Pekingese, but may be hypoallergenic and intelligent, from the Poodle in the mix. These dogs are usually not good with young children because the dogs are small and do not tolerate rough play. For more on the Pekingese and the Poodle, see pages 114 and 115.

Queen Isabella is a nine-month-old Peekapoo. I call her Bella. By the time Bella was a year old, she was completely silver and white. Her breeder had told me that she would be, but I didn't believe her.—Morgan L.

We have bred Peek-A-Poos and have gotten good feedback on this mix. Overall, they make a nice dog that is sturdy and outgoing. Usually hypoallergenic.—Renée B. and Sherwood P.

Poochon

Bichon Frise

Poodle

• DOG DATA •

THE POOCHON VARIES IN SIZE and weight, depending on whether the Bichon Frise is bred with a Toy, Miniature, or Standard Poodle. Both parent breeds are known for their high intelligence, and both are recommended for children and allergy sufferers. For more on the Bichon Frise and the Poodle, see pages 103 and 105.

The Poochon combines the more robust, oblong body of the Bichon with the intelligence of the Poodle, making a wonderful and happy companion. Depending on the color of the Poodle parent, the variance can be wide, but Poochons are most often white in color. They are active, intelligent, loyal, and affectionate. Typically, this is an ideal dog for children. Their size and playful nature make them a family favorite. Poochons are highly obedient and quite easy to train. They will adapt to living in just about any environment. Because of their size, they make excellent dogs for apartments. They are generally very healthy, as the vigor instilled through this cross makes them less prone to the ailments that afflict the parent breeds.—Tammy, Rolling Meadows Kennel

Izzy has the most easygoing, loving, friendly personality. *He also has been great with obedience. We started classes when he was 14 weeks old and have continued on with other ones. We even took a Trick Training class, which he loved. We love the dog park—Izzy loves all the dogs and they love him too. I still feel blessed every day to have him in my life.—Erin; provided from the Rolling Meadows Web site*

Schnoodle

• PARENT BREEDS •

Schnauzer

Poodle

• DOG DATA •

SCHNOODLES VARY IN WEIGHT and size, depending on whether the Poodle parent is a miniature or standard breed. Breeders and owners often referred to the hypoallergenic nature of their dogs (although Schnauzers generally are not recommended for allergy sufferers). Schnoodles may have high intelligence and are good with children. The Schnoodle has gained celebrity status as the preferred pooch of actress Natalie Portman. For more information, see the Schnauzer and Poodle on pages 118 and 115.

Our dog is a female Schnoodle named Cricket. Cricket is 22 months old and weighs approximately 14 pounds [6.3 kg]. She is our second Schnoodle. Our first (Casey) was adopted in 1992 and lived until she was nearly 12 years old. She was born with a heart murmur and died of congestive heart failure. Nevertheless, Casey was a happy and loving companion to the whole family. We were so impressed by the inherent qualities of this mixed breed that we chose another Schnoodle as our new family member. Cricket is affectionate, playful, gentle, and full of love. She likes everyone and has not a mean bone in her body. She rarely vocalizes and will only bark occasionally when she gets excited. As was the case with both of our Schnoodles, they shed very little and are hypoallergenic. Both were very easy to train. They are intelligent, love to please, and become distressed if they think that someone is unhappy with them. I would highly recommend this new breed to anyone.—Dan and Carolyn D.

Maxwell Benjamin Smart (aka Maxi B.) is my two-year-old Schnoodle. He is very spoiled, as he goes to "day care," where they tell me that he is a ringleader for all the other dogs. He weighs 20 pounds [9 kg] and was bought from a breeder here in Texas. He doesn't shed....He is bright and very loving.—Lisa L.

I have a Schnoodle
named Sophie. She is a year and two months old and is sweet and energetic. She is very smart. I love her to death!—Karen T.

We have been breeding
Schnoodles for over six years. They are easy to train, very intelligent, loving, low- to non-shedding, and great for people with allergies.—James and Crystal S.

Shih-Poo

• PARENT BREEDS •

Shih Tzu

Poodle

• DOG DATA •

THE SIZE AND WEIGHT of the Shih-Poo are dependent partially on whether its Poodle parent is a Toy or Miniature Poodle. While Shih Tzus are not easily trained or housebroken, the Poodle's high intelligence and hypoallergenic coat may result in a dog that is both smart and appropriate for allergy sufferers. See pages 115 and 119 for more on Poodles and Shih Tzus.

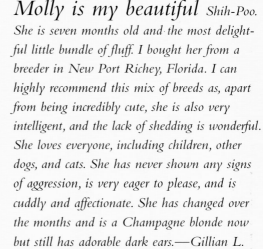

Molly is my beautiful Shih-Poo. *She is seven months old and the most delightful little bundle of fluff. I bought her from a breeder in New Port Richey, Florida. I can highly recommend this mix of breeds as, apart from being incredibly cute, she is also very intelligent, and the lack of shedding is wonderful. She loves everyone, including children, other dogs, and cats. She has never shown any signs of aggression, is very eager to please, and is cuddly and affectionate. She has changed over the months and is a Champagne blonde now but still has adorable dark ears.*—Gillian L.

My wife and I have a wonderful puppy named Stewy. He is six months old and a great companion. He is a little love and likes to give kisses.—Steven S.

Trixie is a little fireball and so much fun. She learned to sit when she was very young in a matter of 20 minutes of training. She also learned to use the doggie door as soon as she was big and strong enough to push her way through and hoist herself up. So, I'd say that she is super smart! She loves to ride in the car, and absolutely adores people! There's not an ounce of snippiness in her, as Shih Tzus have a reputation for. She's really the happiest little thing. She doesn't have too smashed in of a face, and her jaw doesn't stick out at the bottom, like Shihs are known for. Her hair/fur can look a little scraggly, like it doesn't know if it wants to be long and pretty like a Shih, or wavy from the Poodle side. I would absolutely recommend this mix to anyone, so long as their kids aren't too young, as she's only 7 1/2 pounds [3.4 kg] at seven months now, and tends to get underfoot.—Tanya K.

Taco Terrier

• PARENT BREEDS •

Chihuahua

Toy Fox Terrier

• DOG DATA •

THE TACO TERRIER MAY GROW to between 6 and 11 inches (15 and 27.5 cm) in height and up to 7 pounds (3.2 kg), based on its parent breeds. Both the Chihuahua and the Toy Fox Terrier are intelligent and easy to train. Because of the dog's small size, the Taco Terrier might be better for older children. Neither parent breed is recommended for allergy sufferers. See pages 106 and 120 for more on the Chihuahua and the Toy Fox Terrier.

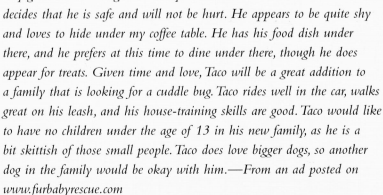

Taco is a very sweet little guy and very good at bestowing kisses on you once he decides that he is safe and will not be hurt. He appears to be quite shy and loves to hide under my coffee table. He has his food dish under there, and he prefers at this time to dine under there, though he does appear for treats. Given time and love, Taco will be a great addition to a family that is looking for a cuddle bug. Taco rides well in the car, walks great on his leash, and his house-training skills are good. Taco would like to have no children under the age of 13 in his new family, as he is a bit skittish of those small people. Taco does love bigger dogs, so another dog in the family would be okay with him.—From an ad posted on www.furbabyrescue.com

Yorkie-Poo
(Also spelled "Yorkipoo")

• **PARENT BREEDS** •

Yorkshire Terrier

Poodle

• DOG DATA •

THE YORKIE-POO MAY RANGE in height from 6 to 9 inches (15 to 22.5 cm) and may weigh between 4 and 14 pounds (1.8 and 6.3 kg). Yorkshire Terriers generally are not recommended for allergy sufferers, but when bred with the Poodle, the resulting Yorkie-Poo may be hypoallergenic, depending on which parent it resembles. Both parent breeds are good with children. The Yorkie-Poo ranges in intelligence from average to above average. See pages 115 and 121 for more on the Poodle and the Yorkshire Terrier.

I am a longtime Yorkshire Terrier *breeder and have bred Boston Terriers for 32 years. If you had told me six years ago that I would be doing any kind of crossbreeding, I would have assured you that I would not. My friend John (a 28-year Yorkie breeder) started breeding Yorkipoos about six years ago. He had to drag me into it. His reasoning was that people wanted this cross, and this cross was hypoallergenic. What really won me over was how healthy the puppies were, not to mention beautiful. Breeding Yorkies is a dedication; the puppies are so tiny when born, and even the best Yorkies can develop hypoglycemia. The Yorkipoos, however, rarely do.—Marlene L.*

We have a six-month-old Yorkipoo named Bailey. She is so wonderful and energetic. She has a Yorkie head and Poodle ears.—Tiffany F.

My 10-week-old Yorkipoo is named Murphy. We got him from a breeder near Diamond, Missouri. Murphy is a sweet and rambunctious puppy that seems to be learning very quickly.—Morgan M.

Zuchon

• PARENT BREEDS •

Shih Tzu

Bichon Frise

• DOG DATA •

ZUCHONS MAY RANGE IN HEIGHT from 8 to 11 inches (20 to 27.5 cm) and in weight from 9 to 16 pounds (4 to 7.2 kg). Both parent breeds are double-coated. While Shih Tzus generally are not easy to train or house-break, Bichon Frises are known for their high intelligence; the Zuchon owners we spoke to praised their dogs as "smart" and "eager to please." Typically, the Shih Tzu is not recommended for allergy sufferers; however, when bred with the Bichon Frise, the resulting Zuchon may be hypoallergenic. Both parent breeds are good with children. For more on the Bichon Frise and the Shih Tzu, see pages 103 and 119.

Although I was told not to *get two puppies from the same litter, I, of course, ignored any and all advice. I am so glad I did…they are the most beautiful dogs I have ever encountered! I have been a dog owner most of my life, and I can't tell you how wonderful these dogs are. They have the sweetest temperament, and are wonderful with my children (all five of them). They are both kennel-trained and house-trained. Smart as can be.*
—*Proud Momma, Donna L.*

Maggie the Zuchon is the most loving, playful, well-behaved, funny dog. She wants to be with you or the family or other pets at all times and she enjoys every minute.—Madelyn

We purchased our Zuchon from a low-key breeder….He has proven thus far to be smart, outgoing, sweet, playful, energetic, and very social. He's friendly to all and has a wonderful disposition, and he has learned to understand several words. He needs to be combed or brushed daily. He loves to retrieve toys and play tug-of-war, and tries to eat whatever is on the ground. This mixed breed seems to be mellow. I have had puppies in the past, and he is calmer. I would recommend this hybrid dog for families with children and for older couples as well.—Christine M.

Gipper is an 18-month-old Zuchon and weighs 16 pounds [7.2 kg]. He is a real joy! He gets a haircut every six weeks, cut to about $1/2$ inch [1.25 cm] all over his body, but we leave his ears and tail long. He does not shed at all, but the long hair on his ears and tail needs combing through every few days, or he has real matting problems. He is smart, obedient, and eager to please....He is very accepting of visitors, and wants their attention, but will leave them alone if told firmly. We socialized him to other people, kids, and dogs.—Paula P.

3

The Purebreds Behind the Top Designer Dogs

In this chapter, you will find an alphabetical listing of each of the purebred dogs that go into the hybrid mixes discussed in this book. Each listing will describe the primary traits of that breed, including size, weight, appearance, coat, activity level, intelligence, personality, and whether or not the breed is recommended for individuals with common allergies. Select the two breeds that best reflect your household requirements to produce the hybrid mix best for you!

Here is a quick list of the breeds described in the upcoming pages:

Basset Hound	Labrador Retriever
Beagle	Lhasa Apso
Bichon Frise	Maltese
Boston Terrier	Pekingese
Cavalier King Charles Spaniel	Poodle
Chihuahua	Pug
Cocker Spaniel	Schnauzer
Dachshund	Shih Tzu
French Bulldog	Toy Fox Terrier
Golden Retriever	Yorkshire Terrier

• DOG DATA •

Basset Hound

AKC Group: Hound.

Size: 13–14 inches (32.5–35 cm) tall.

Weight: 40–60 pounds (18–27 kg).

Coat: Short coat, requires little care.

Color: Black, white, and tan combination, or any other recognized hound color.

Appearance: Long body, low to the ground; head with a long muzzle, prominent brow bone, jowls; long pendulous ears; soft, sad eyes that may be hooded with a loose eyelid; long tail curved and erect.

Temperament: A good-natured and calm dog, good with children.

Basset Hounds require regular exercise to remain fit. They are natural trackers, so they might follow a scent and wander off.

Exercise: Basset Hounds can be overweight, resulting in back problems, so activity should be encouraged.

Intelligence: Average.

Obedience: Average.

Watchdog? Yes.

Guard Dog? No.

Good with Children? Excellent.

Good for Allergy Sufferers? No.

Related Designer Dog: Bagel Hound (+ Beagle)

• DOG DATA •

Beagle

AKC Group: Hound.

Size: 13–15 inches (32.5–37.5 cm) tall.

Weight: 18–30 pounds (8.1–13.5 kg).

Coat: Short coat, requires little care.

Color: Black, white, tan combination.

Appearance: Long head, long ears, long tail, muscular body.

Temperament: Affectionate, gentle, bred for hunting, seeks companionship.

Exercise: Average; can be left outdoors in a pen.

Intelligence: Average; can be difficult to train.

Obedience: Not very obedient.

Watchdog? Will bark at strangers.

Guard Dog? No.

Good with Children? Yes.

Good for Allergy Sufferers? No.

Related Designer Dogs: Bagel Hound (+ Basset Hound), Boglen Terrier (+Boston Terrier), Puggle (+ Pug)

• DOG DATA •

Bichon Frise

AKC Group: Non-sporting.

Size: 9–11 inches (22.5–27.5 cm) tall.

Weight: 10–16 pounds (4.5–7.2 kg).

Coat: Double-coated: dense under-coat and soft, curly outercoat, like a Poodle.

Color: White, cream.

Appearance: Long fluffy ears, round black eyes and nose, looks like a powder puff, short solid legs and body.

Temperament: Sweet, friendly, gentle, happy, lively, cuddly.

Exercise: Energetic, needs daily exercise; can be an indoor dog; should not live outdoors.

Intelligence: High; originally bred for performing.

Obedience: Easy to train.

Watchdog? Will bark at strangers.

Guard Dog? No.

Good with Children? Yes.

Good for Allergy Sufferers? Yes.

Related Designer Dogs: Cavachon (+ Cavalier King Charles Spaniel), Poochon (+ Poodle), Zuchon (+ Shih Tzu)

• DOG DATA •

Appearance: A compact and muscular dog, bred from the Bulldog; flat, square face; pointed, erect ears; distinctive facial and body markings, with a white blaze on the forehead and muzzle; white chest and lower legs; black masklike patches on the face; black covering the body and upper legs, like a coat.

Temperament: Friendly, affection-ate with family, playful, stubborn.

Exercise: Moderate.

Boston Terrier

Intelligence: High.

Obedience: Easy to train.

AKC Group: Non-sporting.

Watchdog? Yes.

Size: 15–17 inches (37.5–42.5 cm) tall.

Guard Dog? No.

Weight: 15–25 pounds (6.75–11.25 kg).

Good with Children? Yes.

Good for Allergy Sufferers? No.

Coat: Short, smooth, requires little care.

Related Designer Dogs: Boglen Terrier (+ Beagle), Faux Frenchbo Bulldog (+ French Bulldog)

Color: Black and white, or brindle and white.

• DOG DATA •

Cavalier King Charles Spaniel

AKC Group: Toy

Size: 12–13 inches (30–32.5 cm) tall.

Weight: 13–18 pounds (5.85–8.1 kg).

Coat: Moderately long, silky; can be slightly wavy; requires frequent brushing.

Color: There are several typical color combinations for this breed: *Blenheim:* Red and white, with even facial markings and a "lozenge" dot between the ears at the top of the head. *Black and tan:* Black with tan markings at the eyebrow level, on its cheeks, ears, chest, and the underside of its tail. *Ruby:* Red (like an Irish Setter). *Tricolor:* Black and white, with tan markings over eyes, on cheeks, inside ears, inside legs, and on the underside of the tail, with even markings most desirable.

Appearance: Round head, long floppy ears set high on the head, sweet face, round dark eyes, short straight back, long legs, long tail with long silky hair.

Temperament: Sweet, gentle, playful, affectionate, friendly.

Exercise: Enjoys outdoor play and walks, but primarily an indoor dog.

Intelligence: Above average.

Obedience: Above average.

Watchdog? Will bark at strangers.

Guard Dog? No.

Good with Children? Excellent.

Good for Allergy Sufferers? No.

Related Designer Dogs: Cavachon (+ Bichon Frise), Cockalier (+ Cocker Spaniel)

• **DOG DATA** •

Chihuahua

AKC Group: Toy.

Size: 6–9 inches (15–22.5 cm) tall.

Weight: Up to 6 pounds (2.7 kg).

Coat: Two varieties: long-coated and smooth-coated. Smooth-coated variety is easy to maintain; long-coated variety requires brushing several times a week.

Color: Any color or mixture of colors.

Appearance: The smallest breed of dog, they are delicate, with a round head, short pointed muzzle, large pointy ears that stand erect, and a tail that can be up, out, or curled over the back.

Temperament: Extremely devoted, this delightful small dog can be a constant companion. They are active and lively, but do best indoors. Some are timid, while others defy their small size with a bold demeanor.

Exercise: While active, they can get their exercise by running around indoors, so they do not require deliberate exercise.

Intelligence: High.

Obedience: Easy to train.

Watchdog? Defies its size with its aggressive, defensive bark.

Guard Dog? Absolutely not.

Good with Children? Yes.

Good for Allergy Sufferers? No.

Related Designer Dogs:
Chiweenie (+ Dachshund), Chug (+ Pug), Taco Terrier (+ Toy Fox Terrier)

• DOG DATA •

Cocker Spaniel

AKC Group: Sporting.

Size: 13½–15½ inches (34–39 cm) tall.

Weight: 24–28 pounds (10.8–12.6 kg).

Coat: Medium long and silky, the coat requires brushing two to three times a week, as well as professional grooming to keep the dog clipped in the distinctive trim.

Color: The three accepted color groups are black, parti-colored (which can be any color combined with white), and ASCOB (which stands for "Any Solid Color Other than Black").

Appearance: A solid and athletic medium-size dog, with a rounded head; long, hanging ears, set low on the skull; an appealing facial expression; straight back, sloped downward; and a docked tail, carried standing or outward.

Temperament: Happy, playful, eager to please.

Exercise: Originally bred as a hunting dog, Cocker Spaniels enjoy romps outdoors but should not be kept outside exclusively. They can also be walked on a leash for adequate exercise. They can become overweight if not exercised.

Intelligence: Above average.

Obedience: Easy to train; it seeks to please its owner.

Watchdog? Yes.

Guard Dog? No.

Good with Children? Excellent.

Good for Allergy Sufferers? No.

Related Designer Dogs: Cock-A-Poo (+ Poodle), Cockalier (+ Cavalier King Charles Spaniel)

• DOG DATA •

Dachshund

AKC Group: Hound.

Size: *Miniature:* 5–6 inches (12.5–15 cm) tall. *Standard:* 8–9 inches (20–22.5 cm) tall.

Weight: *Miniature:* less than 11 pounds (5 kg). *Standard:* 16–32 pounds (7.2–5 kg), typically, but can be any weight over 11 pounds (5 kg).

Coat: Three varieties: short, flat, and smooth; wirehaired; long-haired.

Color: Red, sable, cream, black and tan, brown and tan, gray and tan, fawn and tan, dap-pled, brindle.

Appearance: Known for its long body and short legs, this dog resembles a hotdog and is often called the "wiener dog."

Temperament: Happy, active, enjoys being with people, barks, likes to hunt and dig.

Exercise: Active and likes exercise. Its small size makes the Dachshund ideal for small spaces, but it enjoys going out or spending time in a fenced yard.

Intelligence: Bright.

Obedience: Average.

Watchdog? Yes.

Guard Dog? No.

Good with Children? Yes, with children in its household. The Dachshund might snap at strangers.

Good for Allergy Sufferers? No.

Related Designer Dog: Chiweenie (+ Chihuahua)

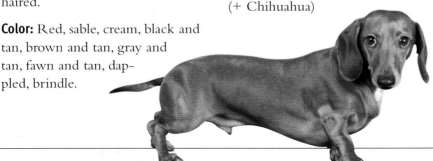

• DOG DATA •

French Bulldog

AKC Group: Non-sporting.

Size: 11–13 inches (27.5–32.5 cm) tall.

Weight: Less than 28 pounds (12.6 kg).

Coat: Short and smooth.

Color: White, fawn, brindle, brindle and white.

Appearance: A small, muscular, compact dog with a traditional bulldog face and erect "bat" ears.

Temperament: A fun and devoted companion; affectionate and eager to please.

Exercise: Not very active.

Intelligence: Average.

Obedience: Average.

Watchdog? Yes.

Guard Dog? No.

Good with Children? Yes.

Good for Allergy Sufferers? No.

Related Designer Dog: Faux Frenchbo Bulldog (+ Boston Terrier)

• DOG DATA •

Golden Retriever

AKC Group: Sporting.

Size: 21½–24 inches (54–60 cm) tall.

Weight: 55–75 pounds (25–34 kg).

Coat: Double-coated, with longer, wavy hair on chest, behind legs, and on tail. Requires brushing two or more times a week.

Color: Any shade of gold.

Appearance: A large, broad skull; short ears that hang down and are set high on the skull; muscular body; strong legs; and a thick, feathered tail, carried horizontally.

Temperament: A wonderful family companion, devoted, alert, exuberant, and playful.

Exercise: A large, sturdy dog originally bred for hunting; some are still used as gun dogs. Others enjoy being trained for field trails, while many others are family companions. They enjoy being outdoors, but they prefer indoor life and interaction with a family. If they do not receive adequate exercise, through being outside or walks, they can become overweight, and they can become destructive from boredom.

Intelligence: High.

Obedience: Easy to train, but they must be socialized as they can be destructive and noisy if not controlled.

Watchdog? Yes.

Guard Dog? Average, because of their size, but generally too friendly to be considered effective guard dogs.

Good with Children? Very.

Good for Allergy Sufferers? No.

Related Designer Dog: Goldendoodle (+ Poodle)

• DOG DATA •

Labrador Retriever

AKC Group: Sporting.

Size: 21½–24½ inches (54–62 cm) tall.

Weight: 55–80 pounds (25–36 kg).

Coat: Short and dense, double-coated.

Color: Yellow, black, and chocolate varieties.

Appearance: A large, muscular dog with a short, thick coat; large, broad head; shorter ears that flop, set high on the skull; kind, intelligent expression; thick tail that is carried horizontally out from the body.

Temperament: Devoted companion, active and exuberant, kind and gentle.

Exercise: Requires a lot of exercise, but can remain indoors if there are adequate opportunities for walks and outdoor play. They were bred as hunting dogs, and are good in the field. They also enjoy swimming.

Intelligence: High.

Obedience: High, if well trained.

Watchdog? Yes.

Guard Dog? Not always, as they tend to be friendly with strangers.

Good with Children? Very.

Good for Allergy Sufferers? No.

Related Designer Dog: Labradoodle (+ Poodle)

• DOG DATA •

Lhasa Apso

AKC Group: Non-sporting.

Size: 9–11 inches (22.5–27.5 cm) tall.

Weight: 13–15 pounds (6–7 kg).

Coat: Double-coated; the ideal coat is long, straight, and hard, unlike that of the toy breeds, such as the Maltese. The coat often grazes the floor and requires daily combing and upkeep to prevent knots and matting.

Color: Any color, including white, gold, gray, brown, and black, or parti-colored with these hues combined with white.

Appearance: Often confused with the Shih Tzu, with which it shares its Tibetan heritage, the Lhasa Apso has a longer muzzle and is typically shown with its hair parted in the center and flowing free. (Shih Tzus, in contrast, are shown with a topknot.) The ears are long and floppy, covered with long, straight hair. The dog is muscular and solid, with a long back and shorter legs. The tail curls onto the dog's back.

Temperament: Active; stubborn; playful, but reserved with strangers.

Exercise: These are strong little dogs that enjoy outdoor and indoor play. While their coats are too long for most athletic endeavors, they still are quite active for their size.

Intelligence: Average.

Obedience: Lhasa Apsos are hard to train and housebreak.

Watchdog? Is wary of strangers and will bark.

Guard Dog? No.

Good with Children? Yes.

Good for Allergy Sufferers? No.

Related Designer Dog: Lhasa Poo (+ Poodle)

• DOG DATA •

Maltese

AKC Group: Toy.

Size: 9–10 inches (22.5–25 cm) tall.

Weight: 4–7 pounds (1.8–3.2 kg).

Coat: Long, straight, silky hair is characteristic of this breed. The ideal coat grazes the floor, and dogs must be brushed daily and bathed often. Show dogs must undergo a painstaking process called "wrapping," in which the hair is bundled in small sections, enfolded in paper, and curled up ("wrapped"). These bundles are held secure by rubber bands, so that the delicate hair does not get damaged or broken. Many pets of this breed are trimmed in the more manageable short "puppy cut," but this eliminates the dog's distinctive appearance.

Color: White.

Appearance: This tiny dog is more solid than it looks, with a firm, boxy body and graceful legs, all concealed by the long white coat. The dog has a round head, a medium muzzle for its size, round dark eyes, and long floppy ears set high on the skull and covered with flowing hair. The Maltese is prized for its sweet and alert facial expression.

Temperament: Sweet, affectionate, companionable, and frisky.

Exercise: The ideal indoor companions, they can be feisty and like to play. They can walk outdoors, but this may be damaging to their fragile coats.

Intelligence: Bright.

Obedience: Can be difficult to train and housebreak.

Watchdog? Will bark at strangers.

Guard Dog? No.

Good with Children? These are small and delicate dogs and are best with older children who understand their fragility.

Good for Allergy Sufferers? Yes. The long hair does not shed if the dog is brushed daily.

Related Designer Dog: Malt-A-Poo (+ Poodle)

• DOG DATA •

Pekingese

AKC Group: Toy.

Size: 6–9 inches (15–22.5 cm) tall.

Weight: Less than 14 pounds (6.3 kg).

Coat: Double-coated, with long coarse hair extending over a dense undercoat. They require daily brushing, and the inverted-V fold over the nose must be cleaned daily to prevent infection. They can also become overheated in summer and do best indoors with air-conditioning.

Color: All colors and patterns.

Appearance: Bred to resemble a lion, this ancient breed was prized by Chinese royalty and was the companion of the wealthy. The breed was introduced to England in 1860, and became a royal favorite in Europe as well.

Eventually, the dogs were bred to be more readily available to all, but the breed requires special care.

Temperament: Outgoing, independent, stubborn, active, and friendly to those it knows.

Exercise: They are more sturdy and active than they appear, but are still the ideal indoor pet.

Intelligence: Average.

Obedience: Difficult to train and housebreak.

Watchdog? Will bark at strangers.

Guard Dog? No.

Good with Children? Not young children; the dog cannot withstand rough handling.

Good for Allergy Sufferers? No.

Related Designer Dog: Peke-A-Poo (+ Poodle)

• DOG DATA •

Poodle

AKC Group: Toy and Non-sporting (Miniature and Standard).

Size: *Toy:* less than 10 inches (25 cm) tall.
Miniature: 10–15 inches (25–37.5 cm) tall.
Standard: more than 15 inches (37.5 cm) tall.

Weight: *Toy:* 4–8 pounds (1.8–3.6 kg).
Miniature: 12–18 pounds (5.4–8.1 kg).
Standard: 45–65 pounds (20–29 kg).

Coat: Wooly, like a lamb's, the poodle's coat must be brushed daily to retain the classical appearance. If the dog is to be shown, there are strict standards relating to acceptable trims, and these intricate designs require professional grooming and regular maintenance.

Color: Any color.

Appearance: This dog has a distinct appearance if trimmed in a show haircut. Such styles include "The English Saddle" and the more familiar "Continental." This elaborate do features a bouffant on top of the head, long full hair on the pendant ears set at the sides of the head, and intricate clipping to create the ball-shaped chest and round puffs of fur at the ankles, hips, and tip of the tail. Many pet dogs will be trimmed in an overall short manner, called the "puppy cut." The dogs appear delicate, but they are strong and athletic. They display a long, pointed muzzle; long, well-formed legs; and a straight tail, held high.

Temperament: Smart, obedient, lively, eager to please.

Exercise: Poodles can enjoy playing outdoors and even enjoy a swim, but they should not be left outdoors for long periods of time.

• DOG DATA •

POODLE CONTINUED

Intelligence: Among the most intelligent of dog breeds.

Obedience: Easily trained and very obedient.

Watchdog? Yes.

Guard Dog? No.

Good with Children? Excellent.

Good for Allergy Sufferers? The best breed for allergy sufferers because the hair does not shed. Loose hair gets caught in the curly, wooly coat, so frequent brushing is necessary to remove dead hair.

Related Designer Dogs: Cock-A-Poo (+ Cocker Spaniel), Goldendoodle (+ Golden Retriever), Labradoodle (+ Labrador Retriever), Lhasa Poo (+ Lhasa Apso), Malt-A-Poo (+ Maltese), Peke-A-Poo (+ Pekingese), Poochon (+ Bichon Frise), Schnoodle (+ Schnauzer), Shih-Poo (+ Shih Tzu), Yorkie-Poo (+ Yorkshire Terrier)

• DOG DATA •

Pug

AKC Group: Toy.

Size: 10–11 inches (25–27.5 cm) tall.

Weight: 14–18 pounds (6.3–8.1 kg).

Coat: Short, coarse hair, which should be brushed occasionally to remove dead hair. Additionally, the breed exhibits characteristic facial wrinkles, which should be cleaned regularly to prevent a buildup of dirt that can lead to infection.

Color: Silver, apricot, fawn, or black, with black mask-like shadings on the face, tips of the ears, and down the center of the back.

Appearance: Descended from the Mastiff, this toy differs from the others. It is a large dog in a small body. It is not fragile and delicate, but active and playful.

Temperament: Happy, playful, stubborn.

Exercise: Pugs require exercise, but they do not take heat well, so they should remain indoors, with air-conditioning on hot days.

Intelligence: High.

Obedience: Easy to train; Pugs seek to please their masters.

Watchdog? Will bark at strangers.

Guard Dog? Too small to be an effective guard dog.

Good with Children? Yes, as they are sturdy for their size and enjoy play.

Good for Allergy Sufferers? No.

Related Designer Dogs: Chug (+ Chihuahua), Puggle (+ Beagle)

• DOG DATA •

Schnauzer (Miniature)

AKC Group: Terrier.

Size: 12–14 inches (30–35 cm) tall.

Weight: 13–15 pounds (6–7 kg).

Coat: Double-coated, this breed requires brushing two or more times a week, and regular professional grooming to maintain the characteristic appearance.

Color: Black or salt and pepper.

Appearance: This solid dog has a distinguished head, with small cropped and pointed ears held erect, or not cropped and folding over the head. They have a long, rectangular head with prominent "eyebrows" and facial fur that resembles a moustache and beard. The dog is muscular, with long legs and a short docked tail.

Temperament: Playful, alert, gets along well with people and other pets.

Exercise: Schnauzers are energetic and enjoy play indoors or out.

Intelligence: High.

Obedience: Schnauzers can be trained to obey, but they exhibit the independent Terrier nature.

Watchdog? Will bark at strangers.

Guard Dog? No.

Good with Children? Excellent, as Schnauzers are gentle, sturdy, and active.

Good for Allergy Sufferers? No.

Related Designer Dog: Schnoodle (+ Poodle)

Shih Tzu

AKC Group: Toy.

Size: 8–11 inches (20–27.5 cm) tall.

Weight: 9–16 pounds (4–7.2 kg).

Coat: Double-coated, with long, thick hair to the ground. Daily brushing and professional grooming are necessary. The hair at the top of the head is pulled into a ponytail that can be finished with a bow. Pet dogs may be clipped short to reduce upkeep requirements, but the haircut eliminates the breed's characteristic appearance.

Color: Any color or parti-colored with white. If parti-colored, a blaze of white on the center of the face is desirable.

Appearance: With its round head and long floppy ears set high on the skull, the Shih Tzu resembles the Lhasa Apso. The Shih Tzu, however, is a smaller dog and has a shorter nose. The body is longer than the dog is tall, and the tail is curled over the back and features long hair.

Temperament: Playful, affectionate, spunky, and stubborn.

Exercise: The Shih Tzu is surprisingly active for its size and requires more exercise than most of the toy breeds. They enjoy active indoor and outdoor play, but should not be left outdoors, especially during warm weather, as they do not tolerate heat well.

Intelligence: Average.

Obedience: Not easy to train or housebreak.

Watchdog? Will bark at strangers.

Guard Dog? No.

Good with Children? Yes.

Good for Allergy Sufferers? No.

Related Designer Dogs: Shih-Poo (+ Poodle), Zuchon (+ Bichon Frise)

• DOG DATA •

Toy Fox Terrier

AKC Group: Toy.

Size: 8½–11 inches (21.6–28 cm) tall.

Weight: 3½ –7 pounds (1.6–3.2 kg).

Coat: Short and smooth.

Color: White, brown, and tan; white and tan; or black and white.

Appearance: Erect, pointed ears; rounded head with a long muzzle; straight neck; straight back; petite with long legs.

Temperament: Terrier at heart: active and spunky.

Exercise: Small, so it doesn't need much exercise, just an occasional romp outdoors or inside.

Intelligence: High.

Obedience: Trains easily.

Watchdog? Yes, will bark at strangers.

Guard Dog? No.

Good with Children? This breed is small, so requires careful handling; best with older children.

Good for Allergy Sufferers? No.

Related Designer Dog: Taco Terrier (+ Chihuahua)

• DOG DATA •

Yorkshire Terrier
(Commonly Known as a "Yorkie")

AKC Group: Toy.

Size: 8–9 inches (20–22.5 cm) tall.

Weight: Less than 7 pounds (3.2 kg).

Coat: Long, straight, and silky single coat that falls to the floor. Yorkshire Terriers require daily brushing and professional grooming to retain the characteristic appearance. Pet dogs can be cut short, but they will lose the distinct Yorkie appearance.

Color: Blue and tan, on the face and chest, and blue over the back and body. The puppies are born black, and develop their distinctive coloring during the first year.

Appearance: Yorkies are among the smallest of toy breeds. Their small size and long hair conceal a compact and sturdy little body. The head is round with a short muzzle; the ears are pointed and held erect, set high on the skull; the eyes are medium size and contribute to the sweet but intelligent expression of the breed.

Temperament: The Yorkie acts large for its size, and is a Terrier in personality.

Exercise: These small dogs retain the feisty Terrier nature and are spunky and active. They can enjoy indoor or outdoor play, but they are not good outdoor dogs.

Intelligence: Above average.

Obedience: The Terrier personality can make them resistant to instruction, and they can be difficult to housebreak.

Watchdog? Will bark at strangers.

Guard Dog? No.

Good with Children? Older children, who can respect the dog's small size and fragility.

Good for Allergy Sufferers? Yes. The fur is more like hair.

Related Designer Dog: Yorkie-Poo (+ Poodle)

CONCLUSION:
The Future of Hybrid Dogs—
Mutts à la Mode or Mutts du Jour?

At this point, I imagine that (1) I have captured your imagination and convinced you that a hybrid dog is the one for you, (2) you have decided that the predictability of a purebred dog makes you more comfortable, or (3) you are now determined to visit your local animal shelter to adopt a dog. You have considered the options presented here and are now equipped to make an intelligent and informed decision as to the best type of dog for your needs.

WHEN I BEGAN MY RESEARCH on designer dogs, I admit that I may not have come from a wholly neutral place. I have been involved in the world of purebred dogs and have owned Scottish Terriers: one that won the breed at the Westminster Kennel Club Dog Show and another that won the Terrier group at the Crufts Dog Show in London. It was my belief that purebred dogs have been carefully cultivated over time, and it would not be in their best interests to promote the deliberate mixing of breeds.

However, while writing this book I have been in direct contact with hundreds of breeders and pet owners, some who support pure-bred dogs, others who are new converts to the world of deliberate hybrid mixes, and still others who believe that the best and most humane place to obtain a pet is from a local animal shelter. (In the interest of full disclosure, my cat was adopted from the SPCA.) It was only after I have had the opportunity to exchange information with this large cross-section of pet owners and breeders that I have evolved in my thinking to embrace the expansion of options open to potential dog owners. Choice is a good thing....

I would not have been so quick to accept this evolution in the world of dogs had I not been moved by the sheer number of hybrid-dog owners who have written and told me that they had owned innumerable dogs before, both purebred and of indeterminate lineage.

Yet, in almost every case, they were convinced that their new dog, a hybrid mix, was the best dog that they had ever had. This was not true for only one particular hybrid mix, nor was there a pattern of a few mixes emerging as the "favorites." This statement was made by virtually everyone who responded to my requests for information.

Goldendoodle

I could not statistically rule out the proportion of ecstatically satisfied customers being the result of an online request for information: In other words, would those who felt neutral about their new dog as compared with others they had owned before be motivated to go online to a Web site to learn more about dogs? Or, would those less happy about their choice of a hybrid dog be less inclined to take the time to respond? So, in the interest of neutrality, I sought out a "control" group of people known to me or to my friends who had owned hybrids. They, too, expressed the same opinion. Virtually every hybrid–dog owner contacted shared the happy conviction that their particular dog was "the best." Owners have weighed in with their reasons for finding their hybrid dogs—both the mixes described in detail earlier and those in Appendix A in the American Canine Hybrid Club's "A Complete List of Hybrid Breeds"—so special. Here are some examples.

Our Pomapoo [Pomeranian + Poodle] Cookie is eight months old. He is the best dog in the world! My six-year-old daughter Hallie is crazy about him.

Our dog Jack is a full-size black Labradoodle [Labrador Retriever + Poodle]. Jack is the best dog that we have ever owned. I will tell anyone who is interested in this breed, you can't go wrong. I don't think we will ever own a different breed again. We have found the best type of dog ever.

My dog is a Sheltipoo [Shetland Sheepdog + Poodle]. She is very smart, well-mannered, easy to train, and loves children. She is good with other pets, doesn't shed, and is also a very good guard dog. She likes to interact with people and play with them. I have to admit (after owning Shepherd mixes, red-nosed Pit Bulls, Miniature Pinschers, and an Old English Mastiff) that she is the best dog I have ever had, and I wish I could clone her.

I have the craziest, cuddliest, and smartest dog ever, and she is a hybrid. Her name is Poki Dee Puppy and she is a Pugshire [Pug + Yorkshire Terrier]. She is a great dog, like no dog I ever had before. She is 15 pounds [6.75 kg] with wiry, crazy fur, and she is so full of energy and so smart that it continues to astonish my fiancé and me. She has wormed her way into my heart with her bright and energetic personality and tireless devotion.

My Jug [Jack Russell Terrier + Pug] Chloë is great with kids, other dogs, and cats. Chloë is a love bug and loves to sleep next to me in bed. When we got Chloë, we weren't aware of the designer/hybrid dog craze. We got her because she was just too adorable to pass up. She was so sweet, and since we like Pugs, she was exactly what we were looking for.

This is Mesa, my Chocolate Lab/Boxer mix [no name for this mix yet]. And I could not recommend the breed enough. She is a great dog, very smart, loving, and extremely energetic.

This is Lucy the Puchon [Pug + Bichon Frise]. We think this mix is the best of both breeds. She is a good size, doesn't shed, and is very playful. She has the personality traits that we've observed in both breeds and resembles the Pug side the most, but does not wheeze like Pugs are prone to, which is a plus.

This is my Yorkipoo [Yorkshire Terrier + Poodle], Cleopatra. Cleo
is the best dog we could ask for. I adore her!

My dog Regal

*is a tricolor Cockalier [Cavalier King Charles
Spaniel + Cocker Spaniel]. Regal is by far
the best dog I have ever owned. If more
people knew about what a wonderful family
dog this particular hybrid is, I am sure it
would be highly sought after. Unfortunately,
most Cavalier owners are none too willing to
breed their Cavs to Cockers. So, I don't know*

Cockalier

*if the availability of this hybrid will ever be large enough to find a market like
the Puggle or Labradoodle. But with your book, maybe that will change. It is
certainly time for the dog market to open up its stagnant mind about breeding.
Thank you so much for taking on this daunting task.*

Why do these owners feel this way? Perhaps it is in reaction to the
notion that this particular dog was custom-designed for them, with
their needs being fulfilled in every measure. Perhaps it is because they
feel that they are part of a trend, and they revel in being the "first one
on their block" to bring home a new designer breed. Perhaps it is
because they have fallen prey to the media, which are promoting this
concept as "the next new thing." Perhaps they feel a little bit of
reflected glory from being associated with a trend supported by so
many celebrities. Or maybe, just maybe, it is because the resulting
hybrid dogs really are that good....

Why would hybrid dogs be "the best" to these owners? Perhaps it
can be partially attributed to the theory of hybrid vigor, which proposes
that these dogs are less likely to demonstrate the genetic defects that
can come from too much inbreeding. Owners' high level of satisfaction
with hybrids could be the result of these animals being healthier
than others they had owned in the past. Another reason for owners'

enthusiasm could be that these mixed-breed dogs may combine the most desirable traits of different purebred dog breeds. If, for example, you admire the personality and likability of a Labrador Retriever and can combine that with the house- and allergy-friendly traits of a nonshedding Poodle, this too could produce "the best" dog. Now, add to that a distinctive and new look—one that will have people on the street stopping you to inquire what kind of a dog that is—and you may just have the formula for success.

Why would breeders choose to breed these dogs? First, and perhaps most logical, is the notion that these dogs are in demand, so to create them fulfills a market need; they will sell lots of dogs, resulting in a large profit. Another possible reason is that to create hybrid mixes, one does not necessarily need to have show-quality, AKC-registered animals. The American Canine Hybrid Club will register a litter only if both parents are purebreds with papers from a qualified registry. There is no requirement for pedigree, or any other information, so the animals may be less than stellar examples of their breed.

Puggle

Many AKC-registered pure-bred dogs may also not be the best examples of their breed, but an educated eye can evaluate how closely a dog or its parents adhere to the breed standard. This is not possible in the case of hybrids because the resulting dogs can look like either parent but will more likely be a random combination of their appearances.

It is this randomness, in fact, that has attracted breeders of purebred dogs to the new concept of hybrid dogs. One in particular admitted, "With my purebred dogs, it's always the same. You know what the puppies will look like. But with the hybrids, it's a little bit of a surprise. Not every one comes out the same in looks or color. It's fun. You never know exactly what you

Maltipoo

are going to get, and each litter is different."

A pet owner weighs in on the same subject: "This is my one-year-old Maltipoo [Maltese + Poodle] Darla. I noticed that there are no Maltipoos…with straight black hair. Before I got Darla, I looked all over the Internet for pictures of Maltipoos and I never saw one like her, so I think it will be helpful for people to see as many possibilities of the mix as possible. I know that would have been helpful to me."

Another pet owner said, "Our dog Bandit is a Pugshire [Pug + Yorkshire Terrier]. Bandit was the only one in the litter to resemble the Yorkie—the others look much more Puglike. We have since seen one other from the litter, and it is completely different from ours. Bandit is about six months old now and weighs 15 pounds [6.75 kg]. The other puppy is about 10 pounds [4.5 kg] or less, and looks like the Pug."

One pet owner says it all:

> Tanner, my Cockalier [Cavalier King Charles Spaniel + Cocker Spaniel] is one year old. Tanner's personality is a mixture of both breeds. He is loving and friendly, but also barks at strangers and can be aggressive if he feels threatened or thinks we are in danger. He is playful but not hyper. The thing that I find most consistent in a Cockalier is that there is no consistency in breeding the Cocker and Cavalier. You can end up with dogs that look like one or the other breed, a mixture of the two, or dogs that are really odd-looking. There doesn't seem to be a specific Cockalier look. Honestly, I have seen more ugly Cockaliers than I have seen attractive ones. I hate to say that because I am a fan and owner of the breed. I constantly seek pictures of other Cockalier dogs and desire to meet other people who own this breed, as I am tremendously curious about the Cockalier, and truly fond of the Cockalier breed. You will never find two Cockaliers who look just alike.

One breeder, when asked about why she would deliberately mix two different breeds of purebred dogs, had a different perspective: "Because the puppies are cute and fun. I find that mixing any breed to a Poodle or Bichon reduces shedding, and the puppies are unlike any other breed."

Other comments from breeders included these.

If you mix two dogs with great personalities, you get a really good dog. I really like my crossbred puppies.

The hybrids are generally nonshedding, good for people with allergies, healthier, and better than the original purebreds. They're good for kids and also for older people because they require minimum upkeep.

You get the best of both worlds. Less shedding. A lot of people like the novelty of it. They're very sweet dogs. They're just good.

The hybrids are pretty hearty and pretty healthy. I keep trying to improve them. With each litter, I learn a little more. I think that "designer dogs" are here to stay. But time will tell....

So, will hybrid dogs be a fad, "Mutts du Jour," or will this trend have legs? (Sorry, I couldn't resist that last one!) Will they be the next new thing, "Mutts à la Mode," and stand up to the test of time? While I cannot look into my crystal ball to offer the definitive answer, experience would suggest that some hybrids will catch on and remain favorites while others will diminish in popularity and might even cease to exist.

In time, with careful documentation and dedicated effort to create the best possible examples of the popular mixes, some of these hybrids may ultimately become the recognized and AKC-registered breeds of the future. Labradoodles have already crossed this boundary in Australia,

Labradoodle

where they are considered to be a highly respected dog, adhering to stringent standards and admired for their success as service animals. One can anticipate the same process eventually happening here.

I believe that the huge range of mixes may be part of a passing fancy. Some breeders are already becoming disillusioned with the more exotic mixes. "I don't breed that mix anymore," explains one breeder. "Very few people seem to ask for them. The puppies are funny-looking, so why should I spend my time and money producing dogs that nobody wants? I'm going to stick to the popular mixes." Therefore, a combination of customer demand and breeder supply will eventually limit the number of mixes produced. This may be a good thing, because breeders will then be better able to concentrate on improving the popular mixes, and this will add credibility to the hybrid concept.

So, in conclusion, is a hybrid dog the right dog for you? Only you can provide the answer to that question. But, thanks to our expanded choices, there are countless wonderful dogs out there, and one of them is the perfect dog for you.

APPENDIX A
A Complete List of Hybrid Breeds

The American Canine Hybrid Club (www.achclub.com) has been regis-
tering the litters of hybrid or mixed-breed dogs. The club is recognized as
the primary registry for deliberately created hybrid mixes, and most breed-
ers of these dogs will register their litters with it. The club maintains records
of every registered litter and therefore is uniquely qualified to provide
information regarding which new mixes have been registered and the
quantity of the litters of every mix as well as the total number of puppies
registered for each.

THE AMERICAN CANINE HYBRID CLUB is also indirectly responsible for the recognized name of every new mix. The club permits the
first breeder to register a litter or dog of a particular mix to create a
name for the new hybrid. All other litters and puppies of that particular mix registered after the first litter or puppy will go by the name
chosen by the first breeder.

Utilizing this information, the club has provided the following
valuable list of every hybrid mix that has been registered with it since
its inception. The club lists the new mixes by the names of the two
purebred dog breeds that have created the new hybrid, followed by
the newly assigned name selected by the first breeder.

The American Kennel Club currently recognizes 153 different
breeds of purebred dogs, with another five soon to be added to the
list, and another 49 breeds in various stages of the certification
process. The AKC-registered breeds can be combined in almost limit-
less combinations to form new hybrid mixes. The list of recognized
hybrids continues to grow as the American Canine Hybrid Club registers about 500 new litters every month, some of them in new hybrid
combinations. The following is a list of the 369 recognized hybrids as
of September 2006 and includes all mixes that were registered with
the club at that time.

American Canine Hybrid Club Hybrid Breeds

Affenpinsher + Poodle	Affenpoo
Afghan Hound + Rottweiler	Rottaf
Alaskan Malamute + Siberian Husky	Alusky
American Bull Dog + Boxer	Bulloxer
American Bull Dog + Bull Terrier	BD Terrier
American Bull Dog + Bulldog	Olde Bulldog
American Bull Dog + Dogue de Bordeaux	American Bull Dogue de Bordeaux
American Eskimo + Basset Hound	Baskimo
American Eskimo + Beagle	American Eagle Dog
American Eskimo + Bichon Frise	Bichomo
American Eskimo + Brussels Griffon	Eskifon
American Eskimo + Cavalier King Charles	Cav-A-Mo
American Eskimo + Cocker Spaniel	Cock-A-Mo
American Eskimo + Lhasa Apso	Kimola
American Eskimo + Pomeranian	Pomimo
American Eskimo + Poodle	Pookimo
American Eskimo + Shetland Sheepdog	Eskland
American Eskimo + Shiba Inu	Imo-Inu
American Eskimo + Shih Tzu	Shih-Mo
American Ori + Pei–Pug	Pug-A-Pei
American Pit Bull Terrier + Bulldog	Old Anglican Bulldogge
American Rat Terrier + Beagle	Raggle
American Rat Terrier + Boston Terrier	Brat
American Rat Terrier + Dachshund	Toy Rat Terrier
American Rat Terrier + Miniature Pinscher	American Rat Pinscher
American Rat Terrier + Pomeranian	Pomerat
American Rat Terrier + Poodle	Rattle
American Rat Terrier + Pug	Puggat
American Rat Terrier + Shih Tzu	Ratshi Terrier

American Rat Terrier + Toy Fox Terrier	Foxy Rat Terrier
American Staffordshire Terrier + Bulldog	Old Anglican Bulldogge
Australian Cattle Dog + Collie	Cattle Collie Dog
Australian Shepherd + Labrador Retriever	Sheprador
Australian Shepherd + Poodle	Aussie-Poo
Australian Terrier + Jack Russell Terrier	Rustralian Terrier
Australian Terrier + Miniature Australian Shepherd	Mini Australian Shepterrier
Australian Terrier + Silky Terrier	Australian Silky Terrier
Basset + Beagle	Bagle Hound
Basset + Boston Terrier	Basston
Basset + Dachshund	Basschshund
Basset + Miniature Schnauzer	Bowzer
Basset + Pug	Bassugg
Basset + Shar Pei	Ba-Shar
Basset + Shih Tzu	Tzu-Basset
Beagle + Bearded Collie	Beacol
Beagle + Bichon Frise	Glechon
Beagle + Boston Terrier	Boglen Terrier
Beagle + Boxer	Bogle
Beagle + Brussels Griffon	Bea Griffon
Beagle + Cavalier King Charles	Beaglier
Beagle + Cocker Spaniel	Bocker
Beagle + Dachshund	Doxle
Beagle + Doberman Pinscher	Beagleman
Beagle + French Bulldog	Frengle
Beagle + Golden Retriever	Beago
Beagle + Jack Russell Terrier	Jack-A-Bee
Beagle + Labrador Retriever	Labbe
Beagle + Lhasa Apso	Be-Apso
Beagle + Miniature Pinscher	Meagle
Beagle + Miniature Schnauzer	Schneagle
Beagle + Pekingese	Peagle

Beagle + Poodle	Poogle
Beagle + Pug	Puggle
Beagle + Shih Tzu	Bea-Tzu
Beagle + West Highland White Terrier	West of Argyll Terrier
Bearded Collie + Dalmatian	Bodacion
Belgian Malinois + German Shepherd	Malinois X
Bernese Mountain Dog + Border Collie	Bordernese
Bernese Mountain Dog + Bulldog	Mountain Bulldog
Bernese Mountain Dog + German Shepherd	Euro Mountain Sheparnese
Bernese Mountain Dog + Mastiff	Mountain Mastiff
Bernese Mountain Dog + Newfoundland	Bernefie
Bichon Frise + Brussels Griffon	Griffichon
Bichon Frise + Cairn Terrier	Kashon
Bichon Frise + Cavalier King Charles Spaniel	Cavachon
(This mix can be registered only with the Cavachon Club.)	
Bichon Frise + Chihuahua	Chi-Chon
Bichon Frise + Chinese Crested	Chinese Frise
Bichon Frise + Cocker Spaniel	Cock-A-Chon
Bichon Frise + Coton de Tulear	Biton
Bichon Frise + Dachshund	Doxie-chon
Bichon Frise + Havanese	Havachon
Bichon Frise + Japanese Chin	Ja-Chon
Bichon Frise + Lhasa Apso	La-Chon
Bichon Frise + Maltese	Maltichon
Bichon Frise + Miniature Schnauzer	Chonzer
Bichon Frise + Papillon	Papichon
Bichon Frise + Pekingese	Peke-A-Chon
Bichon Frise + Pomeranian	Bichon-A-Ranian
Bichon Frise + Poodle	Poochon
Bichon Frise + Pug	Pushon
Bichon Frise + Shih Apso	Zulachon
Bichon Frise + Shih Tzu	Zuchon

Bichon Frise + Silky Terrier	Silkchon
Bichon Frise + Toy Fox Terrier	Fo-Chon
Bichon Frise + Welsh Terrier	Wel-Chon
Bichon Frise + Westie	Wee-Chon
Bichon Frise + Yorkshire Terrier	Yo-Chon
Biewer + Yorkshire Terrier	Biewer Yorkie
Bolognese + Havanese	Dualanese
Bolognese + Poodle	Bolonoodle
Border Collie + Labrador Retriever	Borador
Boston Terrier + Bulldog	English Boston Bulldog
Boston Terrier + Chinese Shar-Pei	Sharbo
Boston Terrier + Dachshund	Bo-Dach
Boston Terrier + French Bulldog	Faux Frenchbo Bulldog
Boston Terrier + Lhasa Apso	Bosapso
Boston Terrier + Miniature Pinscher	Bospin
Boston Terrier + Miniature Schnauzer	Miniboz
Boston Terrier + Papillon	Bostillon
Boston Terrier + Patterdale Terrier	Patton Terrier
Boston Terrier + Pekingese	Bostinese
Boston Terrier + Pug	Buggs
Boston Terrier + Shih Tzu	BoShih
Boston Terrier + Toy Fox Terrier	Foxton
Boxer + Bulldog	Bull Boxer
Boxer + Treeing Walker	BT Walker
Brussels Griffon + Chihuahua	Chussel
Brussels Griffon + English Toy Spaniel	English Toy Griffon
Brussels Griffon + Lhasa Apso	Lhaffon
Brussels Griffon + Miniature Schnauzer	Sniffon
Brussels Griffon + Pekingese	Griffonese
Brussels Griffon + Poodle	Broodle Griffon
Brussels Griffon + Pug	Brug
Brussels Griffon + Rat Terrier	Rattle Griffon
Brussels Griffon + Rottweiler	Brottweiler

Brussels Griffon + Shih Tzu	Shiffon
Brussels Griffon + West Highland White Terrier	Griffonland
Bulldog + Chinese Shar-Pei	Bull-Pei
Bulldog + Dalmatian	Bullmatian
Bulldog + Olde Bulldogge	Victorian Bully
Bulldog + Pug	Miniature Bulldog
Bulldog + Treeing Walker	English Bull-Walker
Bullmastiff + Labrador Retriever	Bullmasador
Cairn Terrier + Chihuahua	Toxirn
Cairn Terrier + Havanese	Cairnese
Cairn Terrier + Jack Russell Terrier	Jacairn
Cairn Terrier + Maltese	Cairmal
Cairn Terrier + Poodle	Poocan
Cairn Terrier + Scottish Terrier	Bushland Terrier
Cairn Terrier + Shih Tzu	Care-Tzu
Cairn Terrier + Westie	Cairland Terrier
Cairn Terrier + Yorkshire Terrier	Carkie
Canaan Dog + Siberian Husky	Sibercaan
Cantel + Cavalier King Charles Spaniel	Cavacan
Cavachon (Cavachon Club of America)	Cavachon
Cavachon + Maltese	Malton
Cavachon + Poodle	Cavachon-Poo
Cavachon + Shih Tzu	Cavazoo
Cavalier King Charles + Cocker Spaniel	Cockalier
Cavalier King Charles + Coton de Tulear	Cavaton
Cavalier King Charles + English Toy Spaniel	English King Spaniel
Cavalier King Charles + Havanese	Cavanese
Cavalier King Charles + Japanese Chin	Cava-Chin
Cavalier King Charles + Lhasa Apso	Lhasalier
Cavalier King Charles + Maltese	Cav-A-Malt
Cavalier King Charles + Papillon	Cava-lon
Cavalier King Charles + Pekingese	Pekalier
Cavalier King Charles + Poodle	Cavapoo

Cavalier King Charles + Shih Tzu	Cava-Tzu
Cavalier King Charles + Westie	Cavestie
Chihuahua + Miniature Pinscher	Chipin
Chihuahua + Chinese Crested	Chi-Chi
Chihuahua + Corgi	Chigi
Chihuahua + Dachshund	Chiweenie
Chihuahua + Dalmation	Chimation
Chihuahua + Jack Russell Terrier	Jack Chi
Chihuahua + Japanese Chin	Chin-wa
Chihuahua + Maltese	Malchi
Chihuahua + Papillon	Chion
Chihuahua + Pekingese	Cheeks
Chihuahua + Pomeranian	Chiranian
Chihuahua + Poodle	Wapoo
Chihuahua + Pug	Chug
Chihuahua + Rat Terrier	Rat-Cha
Chihuahua + Shih Tzu	ShiChi
Chihuahua + Toy Fox Terrier	Taco Terrier
Chihuahua + Yorkshire Terrier	Chorkie
Chinese Crested + Havanese	Crested Havanese
Chinese Crested + Jack Russell Terrier	China Jack
Chinese Crested + Maltese	Crested Malt
Chinese Crested + Miniature Schnauzer	Crested Schnauzer
Chinese Crested + Pomeranian	Chinaranian
Chinese Crested + Poodle	Poochis
Chinese Crested + Pug	Pugese
Chinese Crested + Yorkshire Terrier	Crustie
Chinese Shar Pei + Basset Hound	Basshar Pei
Chinese Shar Pei + Pug	Ori-Pei
Cock-A-Poo + Bichon Frise	Cock-A-Poochon
Cock-A-Poo + Lhasa Apso	Lacasapoo
Cocker Spaniel + Coton de Tulear	Cocker-Ton
Cocker Spaniel + English Cocker Spaniel	Colonial Cocker Spaniel

Cocker Spaniel + English Toy Spaniel	English Toy Cocker Spaniel
Cocker Spaniel + Golden Retriever	Comfort Retriever
Cocker Spaniel + Japanese Chin	Chin-Ocker
Cocker Spaniel + Lhasa Apso	Lha-Cocker
Cocker Spaniel + Maltese	Silky Cocker
Cocker Spaniel + Miniature Australian Shepherd	Cotralian
Cocker Spaniel + Miniature Pinscher	Cockapin
Cocker Spaniel + Miniature Schnauzer	Schnocker
Cocker Spaniel + Pekingese	Cockinese
Cocker Spaniel + Pomeranian	Cockeranian
Cocker Spaniel + Poodle	Cock-A-Poo
Cocker Spaniel + Shiba Inu	Shocker
Cocker Spaniel + Toy Fox Terrier	Foxker
Cocker Spaniel + Yorkshire Terrier	Corkie
Collie + Golden Retriever	Gollie
Collie + Poodle	Cadoodle
Collie + Shetland Sheepdog	Cosheltie
Coton de Tulear + Havanese	Havaton
Coton de Tulear + Pomeranian	Pom-Coton
Coton de Tulear + Poodle	Poo-Ton
Coton de Tulear + Shih Tzu	Coton Tzu
Dachshund + Maltese	Mauxie
Dachshund + Miniature Pinscher	Doxie-Pin
Dachshund + Miniature Schnauzer	Miniature Schnoxie
Dachshund + Papillon	Papshund
Dachshund + Pembroke Welsh Corgi	Dorgi
Dachshund + Pomeranian	Dameranian
Dachshund + Poodle	Doodle
Dachshund + Pug	Daug
Dachshund + Scottish Terrier	Doxie Scot
Dachshund + Shih Tzu	Schweenie
Dachshund + Welsh Terrier	Welshund

Dachshund + Yorkshire Terrier	Doxieshire (Dorkie)
Dalmatian + Golden Retriever	Goldmation
Doberman Pinscher + Old English Sheepdog	Dobsky
Doberman Pinscher + Poodle	Doodleman Pinscher
Doberman Pinscher + Rottweiler	Rotterman
Dogue de Bordeau + Neopolitan Mastiff	Ultimate Mastiff
English Bull-Walker + French Bulldog	Free-Lance Bulldog
English Cocker Spaniel + Labrador Retriever	Spantriever
English Pointer + Golden Retriever	American Gointer
English Shepherd + Dakota Shepherd	Foundation Dakota Shepherd
English Springer Spaniel + Labrador Retriever	Labradinger
English Toy Spaniel + Poodle	Eng-A-Poo
French Bulldog + Pekingese	American Bullnese
French Bulldog + Pug	Frenchie Pug
German Shepherd Dog + Poodle	Shepadoodle
Giant Schnauzer + Standard Poodle	Giant Schnoodle
Golden Retriever + Great Pyrenees	Golden Pyrenees
Golden Retriever + Irish Setter	Golden Irish
Golden Retriever + Labrador Retriever	Golden Labrador
Golden Retriever + Poodle	Goldendoodle
Golden Retriever + Siberian Husky	Goberian
Golden Retriever + Weimaraner	Goldmaraner
Havanese + Japanese Chin	Havachin
Havanese + Lhasa Apso	Hava-Apso
Havanese + Maltese	Havamalt
Havanese + Miniature Schnauzer	Schnese
Havanese + Pomeranian	Ewokian
Havanese + Poodle	Poovanese
Havanese + Shih Tzu	Havashu
Havanese + Soft-Coated Wheaten Terrier	Hava-Wheat
Irish Terrier + St. Bernard	Irish Saint
Italian Greyhound + Poodle	Pootalian

Italian Greyhound + Pug	Puggit
Jack Russell Terrier + Miniature Pinscher	Minnie Jack
Jack Russell Terrier + Pembroke Welsh Corgi	Cojack
Jack Russell Terrier + Poodle	Jack-A-Poo
Jack Russell Terrier + Rat Terrier	Jack-Rat Terrier
Jack Russell Terrier + Silky Terrier	Silky Jack
Jack Russell Terrier + Toy Fox Terrier	Foxy Russell
Japanese Chin + Maltese	Jatese
Japanese Chin + Papillon	Apillon
Japanese Chin + Pekinese	Japeke
Japanese Chin + Pomeranian	Chineranian
Japanese Chin + Poodle	Poochin
Japanese Chin + Shih Tzu	Jatzu
Japanese Chin + Toy Fox Terrier	Jafox
Japanese Chin + Westie	Jaland
Japanese Chin + Yorkshire Terrier	Jarkie
Kerry Blue Terrier + Soft-Coated Wheaten	Kerry Wheaten
Labradoodle + Golden Retriever	Golden Labradoodle
Labrador Retriever + Pointer	Pointing Lab
Labrador Retriever + Poodle	Labradoodle
Labrador Retriever + Vizsla	Labralas
Labrador Retriever + Weimaraner	Labmaraner
Lhasa Apso + Maltese	Lhatese
Lhasa Apso + Miniature Schnauzer	Schapso
Lhasa Apso + Pekingese	Lhasanese
Lhasa Apso + Poodle	Lhasa-Poo
Lhasa Apso + Scottish Terrier	Scotti-Apso
Lhasa Apso + Shih Tzu	Shih Apso
Lhasa Apso + West Highland White Terrier	Westie-Laso
Lhasa Apso + Yorkshire Terrier	Yorkie-Apso
Maltese + Miniature Pinscher	Malti-Pin
Maltese + Miniature Schnauzer	Mauzer
Maltese + Papillon	Papitese

Maltese + Pekingese	Peke-A-Tese
Maltese + Pomeranian	Pomanees
Maltese + Poodle	Malt-A-Poo
Maltese + Shih Tzu	Mal-Shi
Maltese + Silky Terrier	Silkese
Maltese + Westie	Highland Maltie
Maltese + Yorkshire Terrier	Malkie
Mastiff + Rottweiler	English Mastweiler
Miniature Australian Shepherd + Shih Tzu	Auss-Tzu
Miniature Pinscher + Pekingese	Peke-A-Pin
Miniature Pinscher + Pomeranian	Pineranian
Miniature Pinscher + Poodle	Pinny-Poo
Miniature Pinscher + Pug	Muggin
Miniature Pinscher + Rat Terrier	Rat-A-Pin
Miniature Pinscher + Wire Fox Terrier	Wire Fox Pinscher
Miniature Schnauzer + Maltese	Malzer
Miniature Schnauzer + Poodle	Schnoodle
Miniature Schnauzer + Shiba Inu	Schnu
Miniature Schnauzer + Shih Tzu	Schnau-Tzu
Miniature Schnauzer + Silky Terrier	Silkzer
Miniature Schnauzer + Soft-Coated Wheaten	Soft-Coated Wheatzer
Miniature Schnauzer + Welsh Terrier	Wowauzer
Miniature Schnauzer + Westie	Wauzer
Miniature Schnauzer + Yorkie	Snorkie
Olde Bulldog + Pug	Miniature Bulldog
Papillon + Pekingese	Peke-A-Pap
Papillon + Pomeranian	Paperanian
Papillon + Poodle	Papi-Poo
Papillon + Russian Toy Terrier	Cherokee Monarch
Papillon + Shetland Sheepdog	Shelillon
Papillon + Shiba Inu	Shi-Pom
Papillon + Shih Tzu	Papastzu
Papillon + Yorkshire Terrier	Yorkillon

Pekingese + Pomeranian	Pominese
Pekingese + Poodle	Peke-A-Poo
Pekingese + Pug	Puginese
Pekingese + Shih Tzu	Shinese
Pekingese + Silky Terrier	Silkinese
Pekingese + Toy Fox Terrier	Foxingese
Pekingese + Yorkie	Yorkinese
Pomeranian + Coton de Tulear	Pom-Coton
Pomeranian + Poodle	(Pooranian) Pom-A-Poo
Pomeranian + Pug	Pom-A-Pug
Pomeranian + Shetland Sheepdog	Poshies
Pomeranian + Shiba Inu	Pom-Shi
Pomeranian + Shih Tzu	Shiranian
Pomeranian + Silky Terrier	Pom-Silk
Pomeranian + Toy Fox Terrier	Pom Terrier
Pomeranian + West Highland White Terrier	Weeranian
Pomeranian + Yorkshire Terrier	Yoranian
Poodle + Pug	Pug-A-Poo
Poodle + Saint Bernard	Saint Berdoodle
Poodle + Schipperke	Schipper-Poo
Poodle + Scottish Terrier	Scoodle
Poodle + Shiba Inu	Poo-Shi
Poodle + Shih Tzu	Shih-Poo
Poodle + Silky Terrier	Poolky
Poodle + Skye Terrier	Skypoo
Poodle + Soft-Coated Wheaton	Swheat-N-Poo
Poodle + Toy Fox Terrier	Foodle
Poodle + Weimaraner	Weimardoodle
Poodle + Welsh Terrier	Woodle
Poodle + Westie	Wee-Poo
Poodle + Yorkie	Yorkie-Poo
Pug + Shih Tzu	Pug-Zu
Pug + Toy Fox Terrier	Toy Poxer

Pug + Westie	Pugland
Pug + Yorkie	Pugshire
Rottweiler + St. Bernard	St. Weiler
Schipperke + Shih Tzu	Skip-Shzu
Scottish Terrier + Silky Terrier	Skilky Terrier
Scottish Terrier + Westie	Coland Terrier
Shih Tzu + Silky Terrier	Silky Tzu
Shih Tzu + Toy Fox Terrier	Fo-Tzu
Shih Tzu + Westie	Weshi
Shih Tzu + Yorkshire Terrier	Shorkie Tzu
Silky Terrier + Westie	Silkland Terrier
Toy Fox Terrier + Yorkshire Terrier	Torkie
Welsh Terrier + Wire Fox Terrier	Wirelsh Terrier
Westie + Shih Tzu	Weshi
Westie + Yorkshire Terrier	Fourche Terrier

APPENDIX B
Hybrid Breeders Directory

Deliberately created hybrid mixes are a new concept in the world of dogs. They can be difficult to find, if you do not know where to look. One way to locate breeders is to go on the Internet and search for the mix that best suits your lifestyle. Typing that name into a search engine like Google, Yahoo!, Ask.com, AOL, or Microsoft Network might be one way to begin.

ANOTHER WAY TO FIND hybrid breeders is to go onto a site like www.dogbreedinfo.com and click on "Hybrid Dog Info" and then "Hybrid Dogs." There you will find a selection of breeders for many of the most popular mixes. In addition, two Web sites are clearinghouses for humane societies and rescue organizations throughout the country. These sites have search engines for purebred and hybrid dogs to facilitate finding the dog of your choice. You can locate a dog, and save it from homelessness or destruction. Log onto www.petfinder.org or www.pets911.com (or call 888-PETS-911) to be connected with these services. Other Web sites that provide lists of breeders include www.puppyfind.com and www.idog.biz.

I have compiled a directory of breeders who produce some of the most popular mixes of hybrid dogs. It was compiled from two sources: the American Canine Hybrid Club (www.achclub.com) and responses to my request for hybrid breeders on the www.dogbreedinfo.com Web site.

The American Canine Hybrid Club (ACHC) has recommended a number of breeders of hybrid-mix dogs who have registered multiple litters of each of their designated breeds. They are certain to be expecting a litter of your selected mix within a reasonable period of time. These breeders will be designated by an asterisk (★) next to their names.

The directory will also include breeders who had responded to my online request at www.dogbreedinfo.com for breeders of hybrid dogs. These breeders will not have asterisks next to their names.

Another popular way to locate a hybrid dog is to ask local veterinarians for recommendations. In addition, if you know people who have hybrid dogs, you might ask for referrals to their breeders. Some hybrids are also available from pet stores.

As you would when making any purchase, especially of an animal who will become a family member and will be living with you for a long time, be sure to carefully research the breeder from whom you will obtain your pet. Contact several, if possible, to compare them. Here are some things to consider:

- What professional organizations and groups do the breeders belong to?

- Will they provide references?

- Where do they register their puppies?

- Where do they get their animals?

- Are their animals health-checked for disease and hereditary ailments?

- Do they immunize their puppies?

- How many litters/puppies do they produce each year?

- How many different breeds or mixes do they breed?

- What can they tell you about your selected mix?

- Is your choice good with children?

- Is your choice good for allergy sufferers?

- What are the grooming requirements?

- How do they house their dogs?

- How do they socialize their puppies?

- At what age can their puppies go home?

- What do they feed their puppies?

- Do they train their puppies?

- Do they guarantee their dogs to be healthy?

- Is there a health warranty?

- Will they take back a sick or unwanted animal?

Always keep in mind that this is not a spontaneous purchase. Dogs are living, breathing beings that will live with you for their lifetime, and not fashion accessories to be discarded at the end of a season.

Directory of Breeders

Below you'll find the names of breeders from whom you may obtain various hybrid mixes. As mentioned, an asterisk designates a breeder recommended by the ACHC. Following this list is contact information for all the breeders listed. Also, note that breeder contact information and Web sites are current at the time of this writing. Breeders may go out of business or change locations, and Web sites may be changed or taken down without notice.

Bagel Hound
www.achclub.com
www.dogbreedinfo.com
www.idog.biz
www.petfinder.org
www.pets911.com
www.puppyfind.com

Boglen Terrier
★ C. Wallace Havens

Cavachon
Mary Lou & Dani Lou Anderson
★ Ed Van Doorn
★ Connie and Ronald Drescher
★ Cindy Essary
★ Peggy and Don Green
★ Karen K. Grell
★ C. Wallace Havens
Mark and Charity Johnson
★ Cindy Kintzel
★ Deb Meyers
Linda Rogers
★ Karen Veurink

Chiweenie
★ Ed Van Doorn

Chug
www.achclub.com
www.dogbreedinfo.com
www.idog.biz
www.petfinder.org
www.pets911.com
www.puppyfind.com

Cockalier
★ Dawn Coffman
★ Peggy and Don Green
★ C. Wallace Havens
Mark and Charity Johnson
★ Suzanne Wilson

Cock-A-Poo
Janet Ayres
★ Dawn Coffman
★ Elaine Craig
★ Barbara Crick
Michelle Dinwiddy
★ Ed Van Doorn
★ Cindy Essary
Debbie Gorton
★ Peggy and Don Green
★ Karen K. Grell
★ C. Wallace Havens
Mark and Charity Johnson
★ Delmar and Kathy Loe
Nick Messer
Bobbie Nowlin
Renée and Sherwood Palmer
Joyce Smith

Faux Frenchbo Bulldog
www.achclub.com
www.dogbreedinfo.com
www.idog.biz
www.petfinder.org
www.pets911.com
www.puppyfind.com

Goldendoodle

Mary Lou & Dani Lou Anderson
Janet Ayres
★ Elaine Craig
★ Barbara Crick
Dee
Donna
★ Ed Van Doorn
★ Connie and Ronald Drescher
★ Janine Ebel
★ Cindy Essary
Wendy Forwell
Debby Gorton
★ Peggy and Don Green
★ C. Wallace Havens
Diane Hyler
Jeanne Meyers
Holly Miller
Kathy Miller
Linda Mosher
Monica Joy Parker
★ Dyanne Ricker
★ Deb Ring
Gina Robinson
Linda Rogers
Denna Shelton
Helen Small
Sherri Smeraglia
Beatrix Taylor
Michael Wagenbach
★ Sharon Williams
www.doodleusa.com

Labradoodle

Mary Lou & Dani Lou Anderson
★ Elaine Craig
★ Ed Van Doorn
★ Connie and Ronald Drescher
★ Janine Ebel
★ Cindy Essary
★ C. Wallace Havens
Jim and Tam Heckman
Diane Hyler
Shelly Lehr
Richard Martel
Holly Miller

Kathy Miller
Ellis Moonen
Dixie Moore
★ Sharon Munk
★ Deb Ring
Joy Simpson
★ Sharon Williams

Lhasa-Poo

★ Ed Van Doorn
★ Cindy Essary
★ Peggy and Don Green
★ C. Wallace Havens
Mark and Charity Johnson
★ Delmar and Kathy Loe
★ Shonda Madison

Malt-A-Poo

Delphia Brock
★ Elaine Craig
Michelle Dinwiddy
★ Ed Van Doorn
★ C. Wallace Havens
Lynn K. Hilton
Mark and Charity Johnson
★ Donald and Michelle Landes
★ Deb Meyers
Renée and Sherwood Palmer
Bonnie Wagenbach
Norma Westgard
★ Joyce Zwickl

Peke-A-Poo

Michelle Dinwiddy
★ Ed Van Doorn
★ Karen K. Grell
★ Harley Hanson
★ C. Wallace Havens
Mark and Charity Johnson
★ Delmar and Kathy Loe
★ Shonda Madison
★ Sharon Munk
Renée and Sherwood Palmer
Allison Pennington
★ Suzanne Wilson

Poochon
* ★ C. Wallace Havens
* ★ Craig and Ovella Lange
* ★ Ed Van Doorn
* ★ Karen Veurink
* Bonnie Wagenbach

Puggle
* Chelle Calbert
* ★ Barbara Crick
* Michelle Dinwiddy
* ★ Ed Van Doorn
* ★ Peggy and Don Green
* ★ C. Wallace Havens
* J & J Kennels
* Mark and Charity Johnson
* ★ Craig and Ovella Lange
* ★ Sharon Munk
* Shauna Rogers
* ★ Angie Thompson

Schnoodle
* Janet Ayres
* ★ Elaine Craig
* ★ Ed Van Doorn
* ★ C. Wallace Havens
* J & J Kennels
* Mark and Charity Johnson
* ★ Craig and Ovella Lange
* ★ Delmar and Kathy Loe
* Allison Pennington
* ★ Deb Ring
* James and Crystal Schulte
* Sherri Smeraglia
* ★ Suzanne Wilson

Shih-Poo
* ★ Ed Van Doorn
* ★ Harley Hanson
* ★ C. Wallace Havens
* Mark and Charity Johnson
* ★ Donald and Michelle Landes
* ★ Shonda Madison
* Brenda Redell
* ★ Suzanne Wilson

Taco Terrier
* ★ Angie Thompson

Yorkie-Poo
* ★ Ed Van Doorn
* ★ Cindy Essary
* J & J Kennels
* Mark and Charity Johnson
* Sharon Kieffer
* ★ Donald and Michelle Landes
* ★ Craig and Ovella Lange
* Marlene Lippert
* Bonnie Wagenbach

Zuchon
* Mileen Coulter
* ★ Ed Van Doorn
* ★ Cindy Essary
* Carolyn Friesema
* ★ Karen K. Grell
* ★ C. Wallace Havens
* ★ Cindy Kintzel
* ★ Craig and Ovella Lange
* ★ Karen Veurink
* Jeff and Monti Wagenbach
* ★ Suzanne Wilson

Contact Information for Hybrid Breeders in the United States and Canada

Mary Lou & Dani Lou Anderson
Star View Kennels
Mount Vernon, WA 98273
360-422-7603 or 360-391-4603
www.starviewkennels.com

Janet Ayres
Ayers' Pampered Pets
www.ayerspamperedpets.net

Delphia Brock
Farragut, TN
www.brockkennels.com

Chelle Calbert
Designer Doggies
415-999-4114
www.designerdoggies.com
For pet photography
and Puggles calendar:
www.chellephoto.com

★ Dawn Coffman
Misty Trail Kennels
P.O. Box 231
Maynard, AR 72444
870-647-3433

Mileen Coulter
FancyPoo4U
34 Billy Davis Rd.
Silver Creek, MS 39663
601-954-9124
fancypoo4u@aol.com
www.fancypoo4u.com

★ Elaine Craig
Sunset Acres
Rt. 2, Box 31
Butler, MO 64730
660-679-6926
ekcraig@earthlink.net

★ Barbara Crick
Crick's Kennel
46785 828th Rd.
Burwell, NE 68823

Dee
704-278-3647
www.goldendoodleworld.com

Michelle Dinwiddy
Piney Mountain Puppies
334 Piney Mountain Rd.
Narrows, VA 24124
540-726-3334
www.pineymountainpuppies.com

Donna
Doodles by Donna
info@doodlesbydonna.com

★ Ed Van Doorn
Squawcreek Kennel
P.O. Box 20
Barnes, City, IA 50027
641-644-5245

★ Connie and Ronald Drescher
67538 170th St.
Alden, MN 56009
507-265-3257

★ Janine Ebel
31550 108th St.
Herreid, SD 57632
605-437-2460
ebelja@valleytel.net

★ Cindy Essary
County Line Kennels
1906 Hwy. S. 45
Melcher-Dallas, IA 50062

Wendy Forwell
Highview Poodles and Doodles
519-696-2883
www.poodlesanddoodles.com

Carolyn Friesema
Adamstown, PA
cfrie@ptd.net

Debbie Gorton
Debbie's Doodles
32540 Appaloosa Trail
Sorrento, FL 32776
www.webspawner.com/users/
dgorton/index.html

★ Peggy and Don Green
P.O. Box 155
Lavaca, AR 72941
479-674-2467

★ Karen K. Grell
Grell's K-D Kennels
3276 G. Ave.
Vail, IA 51465
712-677-2310

★ Harley Hanson
Rt. 1, Box 149
Scotia, NE 68875
308-245-3284
harsudogs@nctc.net

★ C. Wallace Havens
Puppy Haven Kennel
PO Box 127
Kingston, WI 53939
920-394-2300
Fax: 920-394-2301
pup3090@aol.com
www.puppyhavenkennel.com or
www.puppyhaven.biz

Jim and Tam Heckman
Delaware Doodles
delawaredoodles@mchsi.com

Lynn M. Hilton
293 Sherman Dr.
Crossville, TN 38555
931-456-8996
www.sevenoaksmaltipoos.com

Dianne Hyler
Double D Labradoodles
P.O. Box 1012
Howard, KS 67349
620-374-2103 or 620-330-0859
www.ddlabradoodles.com

J & J Kennels
5406 W. State Road 42
Clayton, IN 46118
317-446-7083

Mark and Charity Johnson
110 W. Columbus St.
Kenton, OH 43326
419-675-3444 or 419-673-1040
yournewpuppy@wcoil.com

Sharon Kieffer
3 Pines Kennels
scoobydoo511@clearwire.net

★ Cindy Kintzel
462 Warbler Ave.
Ackley, IA 50601
641-847-2755
cavachonconnection@yahoo.com

★ Donald and Michelle Landes
5692 State Rt. 726
Eldorado, OH 45321
937-273-2731

★ Craig and Ovella Lange
Sunset Kennels
77 Kent Lane
Silex, MO 63377

Shelly Lehr
Countryclub Labradoodles
661-873-8811 or 661-201-9112
www.countryclublabradoodles.com

Marlene Lippert
Porsche91171@aol.com

★ Delmar and Kathy Loe
Loe Kennels 303 Grant; P.O. Box 205
Jewell, KS 66949
785-428-3315

★ Shonda Madison
Rt. 1, Box 667A Exeter, MO 65647
417-847-5245

Richard Martel
Melorich Australian Labradoodles of Ohio
216-292-6047
Rich@ohiolabradoodles.com

Nick Messer
Flying F Farms & Kennels
40138 Hwy. 71 Berthan, MN 56437
866-336-7023 or 218-738-5189
www.flyingffarms.com

★ Deb Meyers
704 10th St. Grundy Center, IA 50638
319-824-3214

Jeanne Meyers
Pin Oak Farm East Earl, PA
www.pinoakfarm.com

Holly Miller
10331 E. Dutch Ave. Peabody, KS 66866
620-983-2116
www.fourpawsdoodles.com

Kathy Miller
Windchime Kennel
www.windchimekennel.com

Ellis Moonen
Meanderine Labradoodles
R.D. 2 Rangiora South Island
New Zealand
03-00643128862
elmoom@xtra.co.nz

Dixie Moore
Dixie's Doodles
4575 W. Hwy. 29 Georgetown, TX 78628
512-762-8030
www.dixiesdoodles.com

Linda Mosher
Northwoods Goldendoodles
www.northwoodsgoldendoodles.com

★ Sharon Munk
BJ's & Guys
H. C. 1, Box 38 Menlo, KS 67753
785-2251
bjsandguys@hotmail.com

Bobbie Nowlin
Angels Cove Cockapoos
21340 State Rt. 278 SW
Nelsonville, OH 45764
740-380-3655
www.angelscove.net

Renée and Sherwood Palmer
A Tender1's Puppies
560 Harrison Rd. Norway, ME 04268
207-743-1936
www.geocities.com/atender1

Monica Joy Parker
Shady Maple Doodles, Canada
250-337-8910
www.shadymapledoodles.com

Allison Pennington
Integrity Pets
5448 County Road 3214
Lone Oak, TX 75453
903-662-0910
rwenumb@earthlink.net

Brenda Redell
Whistling Wing Shihpoos
P.O. Box 93 Medical Lake, WA 99022
509-998-4042
brendaredell@yahoo.com

★ Dyanne Ricker
Toy Box Kennel
4776 Longley La. Stevensville, MT
59870
506-777-0334

★ Deb Ring
Deb's Doodles
26 Far West Rd. Lonepine, MT 59848

Gina Robinson
Robinson Kennels
47004 U.S. Rt. 20 Oberlin, OH 44074
440-774-4999
gina@robinsonkennels.com

Linda Rogers
Timshell Farm
www.timshellfarm.com

Shauna Rogers
479-638-7421

James and Crystal Schulte
509-299-7725 or 509-844-3980
www.schulteschnoodles.com

Denna Shelton
Doodle Heaven
www.doodleheaven.com

Ivy Simpson
www.labradoodlepuppy.net

Helen Small
Golden Belle Kennels
www.goldenbellekennels.com

Sherri Smeraglia
Smeraglia Teddy Bear Doodles Alabama
251-960-1311
www.teddybeargoldendoodles.com
www.teddybearschnoodles.com

Joyce Smith
Joyces Pups
Roylston, GA
www.joycespups.com

Beatrix Taylor
On Golden Paws
4511 S.E. Clem Rd.
Columbus, KS 66725
bmpuppies@yahoo.com

★ Angie Thompson
Thompson's Kennel
30255 E. State Hwy. N.
Cainsville, MO 64632
660-893-5260

★ Karen Veurink
38046 272nd St. Harrison, SD 57344
605-946-5786
Fax: 605-337-2384
luvmypet@siouxvalley.net

Bonnie Wagenbach
Rolling Meadows Puppies
7671 Stony Hollow Rd.
Burlington, IA 52601
319-985-2189
www.rollingmeadowspuppies.com

Jeff and Monti Wagenbach
TimberCreek Puppies
7575 Stony Hollow Rd.
Burlington, IA 52601
319-752-5331

Michael Wagenbach
Sunshine Acres
P.O. Box 77 Wolcott, IN 47995
www.doodlepuppy.com
Norma Westgard
westgard@accesscomm.ca

★ Sharon Williams
3272 N.E. 100th St. Weir, KS 66781
620-643-5815

★ Suzanne Wilson
Rt. 5, Box 256 Salem, MO 65560
573-548-2232
rswilson@fidnet.com

★ Joyce Zwickl
44995 Rd. V Akron, CO 80720
970-345-2409

Resources for Hybrid Breeders in the United Kingdom and Australia

THE CONCEPT OF DESIGNER DOGS is relatively new in the United Kingdom and Australia. While we provide resources that might be helpful in locating hybrid dogs and breeders in these vicinities, we find that the majority of designer dog mixes can be located more readily within the United States. Most American resources for mixed-breed dogs will be happy to arrange for the shipping of any pet to customers who reside outside of the US.

1stopfordogs.com
A global source for purebred and hybrid dogs.
www.1stopfordogs.com

Animal Registry Unlimited (ARU)
This organization registers all pets and animals, including crossbreeds.
www.friendpages.com/cgi-bin/public/pages/cover.cgi?pageid=animal-registry

Animal Research Foundation (ARF)
This organization registers all breeds of dogs, including new and rare breeds.
www.animalresearchfoundation.com
  Also visit ARF's new European office, Stodghill's European Animal Registry:
http://www.s-ear.nl

Continental Kennel Club (CKC)
The CKC's site has a section called "Miscellaneous Breed Registration," which includes dogs bred from two different purebred dogs (hybrids). This group also has a classified section on their Web site where members can advertise their breeds.
www.continentalkennelclub.com

Der Hund–The Dog–Le Chien
A German-based Web site in German, French, and English; this is the largest European Web site about dogs. It includes advertising for European dog breeders.
www.hund.ch

ePupz
European Web site of dogs for sale
www.epupz.co.uk

International Australian Labradoodle Association, Inc.
A source of information about Australian Labradoodles and Labradoodles, featuring contact information for breeders worldwide.
http://www.ilainc.com/IALA
In Australia: http://www.laa.org.au

International Kennel Club
A source for designer dogs including Puggles, Maltipoos, Shipoos, Cockapoos, Goldendoodles, and Labradoodles
http://internationalkennel.com/designer-puppies.html

International Progressive Dog Breeder's Alliance (IPDBA)
This group unites breeders and dog enthusiasts in one registry service. They register purebred dogs, and will register crossbreeds if they are "registered as the foundation of a new breed." www.ipdba.8k.com

Next Day Pets
Directory of puppies for sale; puppies can be shipped worldwide. www.nextdaypets.com

PuppyFind.com®
This site lists puppies for sale; dogs can be shipped worldwide. www.Puppyfind.com

Acknowledgments

THIS BOOK WOULD NOT HAVE BEEN possible without the help and participation of a great many people. I must first thank Michael Fragnito, my friend and editorial director at Sterling Publishing Co., Inc., because his quest for a Goldendoodle was the inspiration for this book. Meredith Peters Hale is a perceptive and intelligent editor, and it has been a pleasure to work with her again. Edwin Kuo is a talented and creative art director, and I thank him and his team at Sterling for collaborating with us on the creation of this book. I must also thank Jeanette Green and Laurel Ornitz, the managing and copy editors of the book, for their responsibility to the small but essential details that might otherwise be overlooked and go uncorrected.

I am grateful for the time Sharon Maguire of the popular website www.dogbreedinfo.com spent with me. She is very knowledgeable about dogs and provided me with valuable insights into the new world of hybrid dog breeding. I must additionally thank her for placing an inquiry for information for this book on her website homepage. Without this highly visible public request, I doubt that a book like this one could have been possible. She went above and beyond the call of duty by contacting hybrid dog owners and breeders on my behalf, so that I could hear firsthand from a broad spectrum of animal owners. Thank you again for taking the time to help me. Your efforts will not be forgotten.

Garry Garner, of the American Canine Hybrid Club, was another source of valuable information. He generously agreed to open his computer records to verify the popularity of the various hybrid mixes, and then he supplied me with a comprehensive list of hybrid breeders. Without these efforts, this book would not have been possible. I thank you, and I know that anyone purchasing this book to locate a breeder for a specific hybrid dog will also thank you. I also must give thanks to the breeders who so kindly answered all of my questions concerning this new phenomenon in dog breeding. Each of them is included in the directory of breeders presented at the end of the book.

Chelle Calvert, Puggle person extraordinaire and superb photographer, was another essential resource for information, but especially for incredible photography. Your photographs are truly the visual highlight of the book, and I thank you for sharing them with me, and now, with the world!

I'd also like to thank those people who took the time and effort to share pictures and information about their favorite canine companions. While I hope that I have mentioned everyone (and it's a long list...), I wish to thank each and every one of you personally, for responding to my request for photos and information about your hybrid dogs. A great many people commented that they were happy that a book describing and celebrating their beloved dogs was finally being written. I hope that this book fulfills your expectations. I am sorry that I was not able to use every picture received, due to space limitations and photo clarity. All of your dogs are clearly special and beautiful. I sincerely thank you for participating in this project and for helping me to create this book.

Bob Wood & Kelly, Nisha Gabriel & Coach, Marvin Penner & Sammy, Marjorie Kaiser & Bella, Sasha Seely & Milo, Foy Scalf and Shannin Bohnert & Bosey, Samantha Keehn & Jasper, Herman Lemarcq & Achil and Amadeus, Donna Littlefield & Lola and Mia, Gillian Leeder & Molly, Paulette Bennet & Murphy, Amy and Greg Shaefer & Darla, Tim Quinones & Sadie and Lucky, Leaman Antone & Jack, R. Stanley & Lexie, Kimberly Porter & Zoey, Glenn MacDonald & Doobee, Debra DeLuna Goldberg & Baby Bear, Bobbi Jane Flynn & Peanut, Wendy Harrison & Theodore, Joseph Lucia & Wrigley, Elspeth Murphy & Boo-Boo, Angela McDonald & Henry, Morgan Meyer & Murphy, Mary Beth Pekarna & Tori, Ken Lang & Bailey and Brinkley, Lindsay Hogue and Joel Power & T-jay, Atefah Carpenter & Rosco, Benazir Balani & her dog, E. Wyjadka & Jug, Monica Melograna and Jamie Ward & their Gollie pups, Elaine & her dog, Jo Ann George & Madison, Jordis Kummerlander & Mitzvah, Kanisha & Deoge, Lisa M. Long & Maxwell Benjamin Smart, Jennifer & her Goldendoodle pups, Lisa Carlson & Sloopy, Janet Claridge & Lucy, Leyley Stone & Murphie, Sue Welker & her Labradoodles, Nadine Leydon & Sammy, Jeff and Emily Bergeron & Griswald, Tessa Park & Tippy, Jules Sandor & Toby, Varsna & Taurus, K. Widd & Zoey, Leese & Taz and Nola, Denise Mohring & Bentley and Mollie, Cheryl Thibodeaux & Maggie, Jack & Gypsy, Marie Lotty & Red, Lauren Reidinger & Nigel, Jill and Jeff Shaefer & Cosmo, Sheelagh Edward & her Boxweiler, Sara Gross & Lucy, Tenitra James & Kaschew, Amberly & Berkeley, W. J. Jones & Simon, Ianna Drake Rosenthal & Murray, W.C. Bison & Sam, Gary and Rene Lowell & Chugs, Janet Ayres & Chewie, Elissa Sewell & Cashew, Miel Arcari & Peanut Brittle, Kristi McKeag & her Scotland Terriers, Patsy Weaver & her Sniffons, Andrea Raymond & Snickers, Michelle Leighton & Harley Grace, Lisa and Shane Prisk & Tasha, Brittany Lee & Milo, Kawaljit Virk & Rufuss, Kelly Mullen & Twiggs, Krista Deschuk & Cinnamon, McPritz & Samson, Vassi Horn & Jack, Nancy Kelsey & Annie, Malinda Darby & Indy, Nena New & Coco, Miles Kensler & Boomer, Jay Varley & Gordon, Elazar Hoch & Narkadian, Dan and Caroline Dubblestyne & Cricket, Megan Florek & Macy May, Louis and Sloane Smith-Lembo & Olive Ann, Pamela C. Minnix & Rocky, Eloisa Balan & Buster, Lorraine and Ted Beddington & Joey, Angela Sipes & Rufus, Brenda Redell & her Shih-Poos, Nicki McBain Nereson & Cody and Reagan, Tammy Harison & Little Girl, Remmie and Magnum, D'lyn Byers & Pinky, Brittany Velez & Kairi, Chas and Betty Read & Benji, Karina Filiatrault & Milford, Jessica Weir & Solo, Neeja Boyd & Chopper,

Nicole Denterocksnobb & Charlie, Aleasha Casaretto & her dogs, Linda Rogers & her Goldendoodles, Daniel Wimmer & Reba, Steve Jacobus & Kangee, Jacques & Mitsy, Zaid Al-Ardah & Gandhi, Julie Hamilton Hindle & Ace, Christine Powers & Maverick, Linn Torres & Charlie, Lisa Parr-Smith & Beauregard, Caroline Green & Bella, Karen Herndon & Bruiser, Robin Massengill & Buggs, Patric Starkey & Gingy, Barb Jacobs & Reba, Minimeez & Razzle, Barbara Sokol & Bruno, John Korner & Munchkin, Amy Geise & her King Shepherds, Tanya Korzan & Trixie, Linda & Zoe Mae, Audra Miracle & Maggie, Sarah Adamson & Duke, Ursula Hodges & Lady Isabella, Kristina Schafer & Darcy, Kim Johnson & her Brissel Chiffons, Krystal Rene Smith & Storm, Liz Gehrig & her dog, Pamela Gronewold & her Fourche Terriers, Salt & Bugsy, Ashley Liu & Russ, Melody Burton & Molly, Tricia Noble & Chloe, Marcia & Shawnee, Cherokee and Annie, Rhonda Pendleton & Lucy, Andrew Friedman & Maka, Neetu Moodley & Astro, Shelby Dowd & Bear, Leslie & Wrecka and Bruno, Carolyn & her Pug-A-Poo, Pam Owens & Tanner, Renee' & all of her dogs, Michelle Dinwiddie & her Poo dogs, Marilyn Stockstill & her pups, Lyn Chilton and Terry Danford & Scotty Buck, Steven Scott & Stewy, Tiffany Furgason and Justin McCaulla & Bailey, Pepper and Chewie, Amy St. Jean and Cleopatra, Jack Brubacher, Jr. & Struatus, Mitzi Renfro & Lucy, Brendan Kavanaugh & Mesa, Kami J. Loucks & her Coton Frise, Stephen and Cheryl Long & Chloe, Robin McFarland & Coco Chanel, Allison Pennington & Baby, Lisa Ferrell & Sandy, Christine Mott & Bear, Susan Ruth & Cow Fatty, Pamela Monahan & Kalia, Paula Perez & Gipper, Lilie Huynh & Token, Reanuy & Buster, Michelle Jones & Gem, Jenna Rudd & Tonka, Patsy Weaver & Boomer, Erwin Mertens & Tommy, Marlene Lippert & her Yorkipoos, Liz Cho & Lucas, Madelyn Leto & Maggie, Paul Schweinsburg & Daisy Donkey, Alice Ann Allen & Digger, Stan Marsh & Chug, Bunny Patterson & Digger and Coppers, Kristina Stewart & Poki Dee Puppy, Beatrix Taylor & her Goldendoodles, Michael Roedig & Diesel, Maria Garza & Boomer, Cari Naborcyyk & Reesie, Ashley & Hugo, Patrick & Molly and Sandy, H. Stalter & Murphy and Jack, Breann Shea & Lulu, Patty Nolte & Payton, Tina Ruzich & Rocky Balboa, Liza and Rodney & Willy, W. Ursula & Isabella, Brittany Slicker & Penny, Courtney Morales & Toby, Emily Graham & Cody, Mandi Pulliam & Teddy, Karen Tidwell & Lucie & Sophie, Art and Karen Rehn & Annie, Denna Shelton & her Goldendoodle, Littlewood & Teeha and Hooch, Kelley Donnely & Jake, Lourdes Lebron & Tuffy, Linda Hankemeier & Bandit, Denise Klein & Dewey and Pete, Cindi & Jack, John and Kelly George & Penny and Moo-Moo, Pamela Minnix & Rocky, Lynn Hilton & her Maltipoos, Taura Lathem & Regal, Holly & her Doodledogs, Kathy Miller & her Doodles and Poos, Christine Grant & Ruby, Eddie Angelica & Tobey, Ashley Payne & Bruno, Jerry and Karen Edwards & Madonna, Ashley Walter & Sophie, Nancy George & Tai,

Debbie Gorton & Zoe and Lilly, Karin Corby & her puppies, Jennifer Decker & Guinness, Tony Smith & Chaussie, Kelli L. Lowery & her Bulldogs, Melissa Walter & Hugo, Ashley Tantillo and Laurie Hickey-Wynns & their Weimar Doodles, Marjorie Moyer & Bam-Bam, Pebbles and Dozer, Marilyn Bowie & Ricky, Audrey & Lucy, Sharon M. Montgomery & Josie and Riley, Pat Piekarski & Albert, Kristen Atchul & Lola, Nicole & Toby, Michelle Drabyk & Ammo and Mia, Jennie DeFord & Buffy, April Magundayao & Nola, Matt Brandstein & Chuggie, Andrea Alfano & Lucy, Danielle Lee Deans & Darla, Cathy & Rudy, Ashley Hoe & Benji, Amy Reilly & Lily, Nisha Gabriel & Coach, Gavin & Niko, Lucy Bukowski & Bella, Amie Novosel & Cookie, Grace Fisher & Zoe, Ellis Moonen & his Labradoodles, Pamela Owens & Tanner, Ruth Shoemaker & Word, Raysa Ramirez & Precious, James & Crystal Schulte & their Schnoodles, Greg & Andrea Hayken & Arlington, Kate Bobo & her puppies, Steven Branting & Pepper Rose, Angela Hinton & Pudgy, Diane Hyler & Archie, S. Stave & Boshih, Matt Martini & Barnaby, Lou Ellen Lane & Nicky, Lisa Mignosa & Muzzie, Usha Mahabir & Sheila, Mark Munoz & LuLu, Colleen Doyle & Otis, Aaron Jackson & Reggie, Sheila & Saint, Sharon Maguire & Bailey, Carlie Rindlisbach & Bennee, Gina Robinson & her Goldendoodles, Dawn Littlefield & her Sheepdogs, Sharon Montgomery & Riley, Michelle Rogerness & Ginger, Bill Morahan & Brady, Sabrina Bolus & Emily, Derrick and Nicole Williams & Token, Alyssa Smith & Sarge, Donna & her Goldendoodles, Jim and Tam Heckman & their Labradoodles, Jon & Oscar, George & Moo Moo, Kathy Kalaitzis & Tyson, Stefanie White & her Shorkies, Jamie and Monica Melograna-Ward & their Gollies, Charity Johnson & her puppies, Diane & Cookie, Bobbie Nowlin & her Cockapoos, Tricia Freeman & Mr. Lee, Christel Larsson & her Bich-Poos and Yorkie-Poos, Karen Markel & her Sibercaans, Mitchell and Sharon Hipsley & Bell, Norma Westgard & her Maltipoos, Kelly Drinkwater & Jasmine, Dixie Moore & her Labradoodles, Linda Mosher & her Goldendoodles, Monica Parkin & her Goldendoodles, Helen Small & her Goldendoodles, Reneé Banovich and Sherwood Palmer & their puppies, Delphia Brock & her Maltipoos, Wendy Forwell & her Goldendoodles, Trish Shears & Bocker, Daisy and Jazmine, Sharon Kieffer & her puppies, Rich Martell & his Labradoodles, Michael Wagenbach & his Goldendoodles, Dee & her Goldendoodles, Brenda Redell & her Shih-Poos, Jeff and Monti Wagenbach & their Shih-Chons, Bonnie Wagenbach & her puppies, Patsy Weaver & her Sniffons, Shelly Lehr & her Labradoodles, Mary Lou and Dani Lou Anderson & their puppies, Mileen Coulter & her Zuchons, Joyce Smith & her Cockapoos, Ivy Simpson & her Labradoodles, Donna O'Neill & her Miniature Australian Sheepdogs, Janet Ayres & her Poo and Doodle dogs, J. Purcell & puppies, Holly Miller & her Doodle dogs, Nick Messer & his Cockapoos.

Index

Note: Index includes references to breeds featured in the text.
For a complete list of breeds, see Appendix A.

About the Author

ILENE HOCHBERG is an internationally bestselling author whose parody books help millions of people laugh over the absurdities of life and enjoy healthier times with more success and less stress. It's been said that laughter is the best medicine....

Her examination of the anthropomorphism of animals (i.e., treating our pets as people) has been met with great acclaim. The books *Dogue, Catmopolitan, Vanity Fur, Forbabes, Good Mousekeeping, Who Stole My Cheese?!!,* and *Stylish Knits for Dogs* are perennial favorites and have been featured in various media, including CNN, *Good Morning America, Jeopardy, Fox News, Newsweek, Forbes,* the *Wall Street Journal, Vanity Fair, Good Housekeeping, Cosmopolitan,* and *Publishers Weekly.*

Ms. Hochberg's education includes a B.S. in Design and Environmental Analysis from Cornell University. She is a member of Mensa, a former director of fashion and visual merchandising for several well-known stores, has been an instructor at the Parsons School of Design, holds a Black Belt in shopping, and is a confirmed knitter. She has shared her life with a succession of beloved canine companions and is the proud parent of her new stepdog, Kelly, an 11-year-old Miniature Dachshund. In other words, she is the ideal person to have written this book.